A TREATISE ON THE LAW OF INSURANCE

A TREATISE ON THE LAW OF INSURANCE

Dheeraj Razdan

CYBER TECH PUBLICATIONS
4264/3, Ansari Road, Daryaganj, New Delhi-110002 (India)
Ph.: 011-23244078. Fax: 011-23280028
E-Mail: cyberpublicationsdelhi@yahoo.com

A TREATISE ON THE LAW OF INSURANCE

Dheeraj Razdan

First Edition 2009

Published by :

G.S. Rawat for **Cyber Tech Publications**
4264/3, Ansari Road, Daryaganj, New Delhi-110002 (India)
Ph.: 011-23244078. Fax: 011-23280028
E-Mail: cyberpublicationsdelhi@yahoo.com

Printed at : **Amit Enterprises, Maujpur, Delhi, (9810878184)**

Preface

The purpose of this book is to provide lenders, attorneys, regulators, developers, investors, and other professionals with a complete set of both basic and highly sophisticated forms that can be used as practical working tools for various banking and lending-related transactions. The forms contained in this book were gathered from all over the United States from leading law firms, banks, savings and loans, commercial finance and leasing companies, and other similar institutions. Some forms have their own editorial notes as well. These editorial comments and notes discuss general considerations and do not refer to the laws of any one state. It is our intention that the forms serve only as guidelines and illustrations. Readers are cautioned against copying any form without the advice of local legal counsel, since the laws governing the transactions described in the forms frequently vary from one jurisdiction to the next. These four volumes are updated on a regular basis, providing forms of interest based on current developments in the lending community.

Good draftsmanship is extremely important in all lending transactions because of the need to comply with a myriad laws and regulations governing every transaction. The most meticulous care must be exercised to express, clearly and unambiguously, the specific details of the parties' agreement and, in the case of most lenders, to err on the side of conservatism. The forms in these volumes have been designed to alert the practitioner to the most serious and prevalent drafting problems, and to suggest the techniques by which such problems may be fully resolved.

—Author

CONTENTS

1

INSURANCE CONTRACT LAW

PURPOSE AND CONTENT

The teams working on the insurance contract law review at the English and Scottish Law Commissions intend to issue jointly a short series of Issues Papers. These papers are not subject to formal scrutiny by Commissioners and their contents should not be quoted as representing the views of either Commission.

Our intention is that these Issues Papers will promote discussion of some of the main matters within the review, and give a focus for debate at seminars that we are holding. This paper, the first in the series, looks at misrepresentation and nondisclosure by the insured. It also considers basis of the contract clauses, which could currently be used to avoid our proposals.

We consider the position of consumers before we consider that of businesses. This is partly because the law is regarded as having the potential for particular harshness in the consumer context, partly because statutory regulation and an Ombudsman scheme apply to consumer insurance and partly because where consumers are concerned alternative approaches to dealing with nondisclosure and misrepresentation have already been tried and tested. We then move on to assess the extent to which rules which are suitable for consumers could also be suitable for businesses. Finally we consider how small businesses should be treated and, if necessary, defined.

TENTATIVE CONCLUSIONS AND PROPOSALS

No fixed decisions have been reached. Here we list our tentative conclusions and proposals. These will be reviewed in the light of submissions we receive and discussions at the planned seminars. In areas where we have not yet formulated a tentative view, we ask questions.

Consumers

We conclude that the time has come to state clearly what rights and obligations a consumer insured should have. We believe strongly that a new statute should replace the current patchwork by a single system that is coherent and clear, and that is fair in that it meets the reasonable expectations of both consumers and insurers. (para 5.25)

We tentatively propose that:

(1) It should not be possible to contract out of the new rules governing consumer insurance except in favour of the consumer. (para 6.3)

(2) Insurers should only be entitled to a remedy for an insured's nondisclosure or misrepresentation in so far as this is material, as defined below. The same test should apply to misrepresentation and nondisclosure.

(3) First, the actual insurer must show inducement, in that had it known the true facts it would not have entered into the same contract on the same terms or at all.

(4) Additionally, the insurer must show either:

(i) that the proposer appreciated that the fact in question would have that significance or, if not,

(ii) that a reasonable insured in the circumstances would have appreciated its significance.

(5) In assessing what a reasonable insured would appreciate, the courts should take into account the type of policy, the way the policy was advertised and sold, and the normal characteristics of consumers in the market. However, they would not look at individual circumstances, known only to the insured.

We ask whether the test should also take into account any particular characteristics or circumstances affecting the insured, so far as these were known to the insurer. (paras 6.306.32)

We tentatively propose that:

(1) Insurers should be allowed to avoid policies where the insured has acted fraudulently at the precontractual stage, that is, if the insured:

(a) knew that the statement was untrue (or realised that it might be not be true and did not care) and

(b) knew that the statement was material to the insurer (or realised that it might be material and did not care whether it was or not). (para 6.39)

(2) If the consumer insured had reasonable grounds for believing the truth of what they said, or was not negligent in other ways (such as in failing to answer a question), the insurer should have no remedy for misrepresentation or nondisclosure. (para 6.50)

If the consumer proposer has made a negligent misrepresentation, the court should apply a proportionate remedy by asking what the insurer would have done had it known the true facts. In particular:

(a) Where an insurer would have excluded a particular type of claim, the insurer should not be obliged to pay claims that would fall within the exclusion~

(b) Where an insurer would have declined the risk altogether, the claim may be refused~

(c) Where an insurer would have charged more, the claim should be reduced proportionately to the underpayment of premium. (para 6.79)

There are three further issues on which we would welcome advice:

(1) Is there a case for granting the courts or ombudsman some discretion to prevent avoidance where the insurer would have declined the risk but the policyholder's fault is minor, and other insurers would have accepted the risk at a higher premium? This may also apply where the misrepresented fact is unrelated to the claim.

(2) Should insurers be entitled to avoid policies for the future in all cases, or only where they would have declined the risk?

(3) Is it desirable to give greater protection to third parties in the event of misrepresentation by a policyholder? (para 6.81)

Our tentative proposal is that in the consumer market, insurers should ask consumers clear questions about any matter that is material to them and that, if they do not ask questions on a particular point, the insurer should be regarded as having waived its right to such information. (para 6.89)

Our tentative view is that:

(1) General questions should be permitted, but that the court should ask whether a reasonable consumer would understand that this question was asking about this particular information. (para 6.97)

(2) An insurer should have no right to rely on nonfraudulent misrepresentations made at renewal

in response to such a question, unless the policyholder was supplied with copies of any information previously provided to the insurer. (para 6.101)

(3) "Basis of the contract" clauses, whether in the proposal form or the contract itself, should be ineffective to make all the answers given by the insured into warranties. (This is without prejudice to the decision whether or not to permit specific warranties of existing fact contained within the contract.) (para 6.104)

We tentatively propose that:

(1) An insurer should not be allowed to rely on a failure to disclose or a misrepresentation because of an incomplete answer, if the insured reasonably thought that the insurer would investigate and verify the matter. (para 6.112)

(2) An insurer should be treated as knowing information contained in its own files, provided that the information was reasonably identifiable. (para 6.115)

(3) An insurer who has indicated that it may obtain information from a third party (by, for example, asking the insured for consent to obtain it) should not be allowed to rely on a nonfraudulent misrepresentation (or failure to disclose) if the insured reasonably thought the insurer would check with the third party. (para 6.117)

We tentatively propose that insurers should be precluded from relying on a nondisclosure or misrepresentation when a question in a proposal form that requires an answer has not been answered or has an obviously incomplete answer. (para 6.125)

We ask whether in consumer life assurance the insurer should be prevented from relying on any nonfraudulent misrepresentation after the policy has been in force for three years. (para 6.129)

Businesses

We tentatively propose that:

(1) The law affecting business insurance should be changed to give the insured certain additional rights, but that the rules should in general not be mandatory. (para 7.38)

(2) The duty of disclosure should continue to apply to business insurance contracts in general. (para 7.45)

(3) A reasonable insured test of materiality should apply to all business insurance. (para 7.59)

(4) There is no case for restricting the insurer's right to avoid the policy (and therefore to refuse to pay any claim) where a business insured has behaved fraudulently. (para 7.62)

(5) When a business insured has acted without negligence in making an incorrect statement or in other ways (such as failing to answer a question), the insurer should have no right to avoid the policy or to refuse to pay a claim under it on that ground. (para 7.66)

We ask:

(1) Whether the remedy for negligent misrepresentation should be proportionate, in that it should aim to put the insurer into the position it would have been in had it known the true circumstances. (para 7.71)

(2) Whether the insured should have to show that it did not know what a person in its position would be expected to know, or alternatively that it did not know why an inaccurate response to a clear question was material. (para 7.75)

(3) Whether where the insurer would have declined the risk, but the policyholder's fault is minor and other insurers would have accepted the risk at a higher premium, the court should have a discretion to apply a proportionality solution. (para 7.78)

We tentatively propose:

(1) That negligent misrepresentation or nondisclosure should be a ground on which the insurer may cancel the policy after reasonable notice, without prejudice to claims that have arisen or arise within the notice period. (para 7.80)

(2) That there should be a mandatory rule that incorrect answers would not give rise to a remedy for breach of warranty unless there was a term to that effect in the contract itself, rather than merely a "basis of the contract" clause in the proposal form. (para 7.83)

(3) That our earlier proposals for business insurance should apply to MAT. (para 7.87)

Our tentative conclusion is that we should not extend the existing rights of third parties where there is negligent misrepresentation by the policyholder, but we welcome views on this issue. (para 7.92)

We ask if there is any reason not to apply our earlier proposals for business insurance to reinsurance. (para 7.95)

Small Businesses

We ask:

(1) To what extent small businesses should be treated in the same way as consumers. (para 7.104)

(2) How small businesses should be defined for this purpose. (para 7.105)

2

CONSULTATION PAPER

We would very much value your views on these issues. The comments we receive will be taken into account as we draft our formal proposals, which will be published in a Consultation Paper in summer 2007.

INTRODUCTION

The English and Scottish Law Commissions are conducting a joint review of insurance contract law. This review covers both general and longterm insurance, and both commercial and consumer policies.

It is intended that any reforms we recommend will result in the same law applying to England and Wales and to Scotland. Insurance contract law is broadly similar in the two jurisdictions. However, there are important differences. For example, Scots law provides a different test of materiality for life insurance, looking at the issue from the point of view of a reasonable insured, rather than that of the "prudent underwriter".

In January 2006 we issued a Scoping Paper, explaining that the review would examine the law of misrepresentation, nondisclosure and breach of warranty.

We asked whether any other topics also needed to be considered. In the light of the responses received, we will be reviewing most of the areas referred to in the Scoping

Paper. A paper setting out our decisions on scope and including extracts from the responses we received is available on our websites.

We intend to publish a first formal consultation paper in summer 2007. Before then, we are developing our ideas through a short series of issues papers. This is the first such paper, dealing with misrepresentation and nondisclosure by the insured. It also deals briefly with "basis of the contract" clauses. The next paper will consider these in more detail, and also with specific warranties of existing facts and warranties as to the future. We regard these issues as being at the very heart of the review.

Some questions will be considered at a later stage. These include the insurer's duty of good faith the way that the law treats nondisclosure by one party in joint policies and how to deal with disclosures to an intermediary that have not been communicated to the insurer. They are relevant to this topic but considerations of space and time preclude covering them in this paper.

STATUS OF ISSUES PAPERS

This paper has been drafted by the teams working on the project at the English and Scottish Law Commissions. It has not been subject to formal scrutiny by Commissioners and does not represent fixed policy. This paper, together with subsequent papers, is simply intended to promote discussion before the formal consultation process begins. It should not be quoted as representing the views of either Commission.

Our final report will be accompanied by an impact assessment of any recommendations we make. We do not intend to include such an assessment in any of our issues papers, given that such papers merely indicate our provisional thoughts. Nevertheless, we would be interested to hear views on the practical implications of the changes we are suggesting.

PREVIOUS REPORTS

Insurance law has been widely criticised by the judiciary, by practitioners, by academics and others. There have been reports calling for reform since 1957. In our early work we have found three reports to be of particular assistance.

In 1980 the English Law Commission published a report in which it considered two aspects of insurance law nondisclosure and breach of warranty. It concluded that: The law relating to nondisclosure and breach of warranty is undoubtedly in need of reform, and this reform has been too long delayed.

We have found this report valuable, and consider its recommendations further in Part 3 below. However, the 1980 report was more limited in scope than the review we are now conducting. In particular:

(1) It did not consider Scots law.

(2) It was limited to nondisclosure, misrepresentation and breach of warranty. By contrast, our current review will be considering a wider range of topics.

(3) It excluded Marine, Aviation and Transport ("MAT") insurance from its recommendations. We are including them in the scope of our review.

(4) It only considered misrepresentation and nondisclosure by the insured.

We will also be looking at misrepresentation and nondisclosure by the insurer, though these areas will be dealt with in a later issues paper.

Furthermore, some parts of the 1980 report are now dated. For example, the report preceded the opening of the Insurance Ombudsman Bureau ("IOB") in March 1981. We have looked carefully at how the Financial Ombudsman Service ("FOS") — successor to the IOB — approaches these issues, and have tried to reflect the best elements of ombudsman practice into our proposals.

In 1997 the National Consumer Council investigated the operation of the law and selfregulation to identify what it termed "areas where consumers are manifestly still at risk". It said:

> We conclude that the only effective solution to some of the serious problems encountered by consumers when it comes to buying personal insurance is legislative reform.

In 2002 the British Insurance Law Association examined those areas of law which it felt were causing concern in the insurance market and in insurance disputes. Its report, which has been described by Lord Justice Longmore as "balanced and impressive", stated:

> We are satisfied that there is a need for reform.

These three reports present a compelling case for a review and offer a range of potential solutions that are worth considering.

We have also been influenced by the different legal rules applied in other jurisdictions and the reforms introduced in Australia and France.

CONTENTS

The remainder of this paper is split into the following parts:

(1) In Part 2 we set out the current law.

(2) In Part 3 we look at how the strict legal rules have been supplemented by Statements of Practice issued by the Association of British Insurers ("ABI"), Rules issued by the Financial Services Authority ("FSA")

and guidance issued by the FOS. We also consider some of the reports that have been published criticising the law.

(3) In Part 4 we consider the current position of consumers – taking into account both the law and the measures described in Part 3.

(4) In Part 5 we set out the case for reforming insurance contract law as it applies to consumers.

(5) In Part 6 we give tentative proposals for the reform of insurance contract law as it applies to consumers.

(6) In Part 7 we set out the case for reforming insurance contract law as it applies to businesses and give our tentative proposals.

These parts are followed by six appendices:

(1) We outline how misrepresentation is dealt with under the general law of contract – first in England and Wales, and secondly in Scotland.

(2) Appendix B contains copies of the ABI Statement of LongTerm Insurance Practice and the now repealed ABI Statement of General Insurance Practice.

(3) Appendix C contains a brief commentary on the relevant provisions of the ABI Statements.

(4) Appendix D contains guidance from the ABI entitled Application Form Design for Life and Health Protection Insurances.

(5) Appendix E contains extracts from the FSA Conduct of Business and Insurance Conduct of Business Sourcebooks.

(6) Appendix F contains a brief commentary on the relevant Rules within those Sourcebooks.

(7) Appendix G deals with comparative law. It summarises how the issues of misrepresentation and

nondisclosure are dealt with in Australia, New York, France and Norway.

THE CURRENT LAW

In this Part we describe the current law. First we explain that insurance contracts are regarded as having a special status, in that the parties are expected to act "with utmost good faith". Then we look at the law of misrepresentation followed by the duty to disclose.

UTMOST GOOD FAITH

An insurance policy is one of a small number of types of contract that are *uberrimae fides* of the utmost good faith.

For the purposes of this paper, we are interested solely in the impact of the duty at the precontractual stage, that is, before the contract has been formally concluded. As in law each renewal is a separate contract, the duty of disclosure also arises each time an insurance policy is renewed. We will consider the postcontractual duty of good faith in a later paper. The common law

At the precontractual stage, the effect of the duty of utmost good faith is that each party has obligations:

(1) To refrain from misrepresenting material facts, and

(2) To disclose material facts even if no question is asked.

In contrast, ordinary commercial contracts start from the premise of *caveat emptor* – let the buyer beware. A party to a contract *caveat emptor* must not misrepresent facts, but is under no obligation to disclose facts about which it is not asked.

RECIPROCITY

The duty of utmost good faith lies on each party to a policy of insurance. Lord Mansfield's judgment in *Carter v*

Boehm is the clearest early statement that the duty is reciprocal:

> Good faith forbids either party, by concealing what he privately knows to draw the other into a bargain from his ignorance of the fact, and his believing the contrary.

However, in the past, the information relevant to the assessment of a risk has most commonly been in the knowledge of the applicant for insurance. This was recognised by Lord Mansfield:

> Insurance is a contract upon speculation. The special facts, upon which the contingent chance is to be computed, lie most commonly in the knowledge of the insured only: the underwriter trusts to his representation, and proceeds upon confidence that he does not keep back any circumstance in his knowledge, to mislead the underwriter into a belief that the circumstance does not exist, and to induce him to estimate the risque, as if it did not exist.

The result has been that the duty has developed unevenly, so that it lies significantly more heavily on the applicant for insurance than on the insurer. This paper deals only with the duty on the insured. The duty on the insurer will be dealt with in a later paper.

Lord Mansfield's comments date from 1766, when insurers had access to fewer sources of information and when communications were very much slower than today. In some respects the balance of knowledge between insured and underwriter has changed markedly in the last 250 years.

REMEDY FOR BREACH

As a matter of law, a breach of the precontractual duty of utmost good faith will give the other party the right to avoid the policy "ab initio". This right must be exercised within a reasonable period after discovery of the breach. Until such time as the policy is avoided, it is valid and binding. On avoidance it is set aside as from outset – in other words, it is treated as if it never existed. This is so regardless of whether the breach was fraudulent, negligent or entirely innocent. Many allegations of a breach arise after a claim has been made. If a policy is avoided, any such claim may be rejected and any payments already made to the policyholder can be recovered.

The Marine Insurance Act 1906

The Marine Insurance Act 1906 ("MIA 1906") partially codified the common law. Though strictly concerned only with marine insurance, many of its provisions are presumed to be equally applicable to other types of insurance:

Although the issues arise under a policy of nonmarine insurance it is convenient to state them by reference to the Marine Insurance Act 1906 since it has been accepted in argument, and is indeed laid down in several authorities, that in relevant respects the common law relating to the two types of insurance is the same, and that the Act embodies a partial codification of the common law.

Section 17 of the MIA 1906 confirms that the duty of utmost good faith applies to both parties, and indicates the consequences of breach: A contract of marine insurance is a contract based upon the utmost good faith, and, if the utmost good faith be not observed by either party, the contract may be avoided by the other party.

MISREPRESENTATION

Misrepresentation and nondisclosure are often pleaded and considered together. The law of nondisclosure has tended to dominate, with relatively little attention being applied to misrepresentation in an insurance context: Historically misrepresentation in the strict sense has not been of particular importance in the insurance context. This is partly because the extreme width of the duty to disclose material facts, as described below, has meant that often nondisclosure has subsumed questions of misrepresentation. Cases have frequently failed to distinguish between the two defences taken by an insurer, and indeed it appears to be standard practice for an insurer, where possible, to plead both defences.

The difference between the two has been described as follows: In general, nondisclosure means that you have failed to disclose something which was not the subject of a question but which was known to you and which you ought to have considered for yourself would be material, whereas a representation is something directly said in answer to a specific question, and in the present case there can be no reasonable doubt that, if in answer to the question "Has a person who is going to drive the car been convicted of an offence?" you answer "No," you are making a direct representation that such person has not been convicted.

The practical significance of this distinction, as illustrated by the *Zurich General Accident* case, is that misrepresentation of a material fact will afford grounds for avoidance of the policy whether or not the proposer was aware that it was incorrect, whereas avoidance for nondisclosure will be restricted to facts of which the proposer was aware and which they ought to have realised the insurer would regard as material.

In the consumer area, most insurers ask set questions. The cases brought before the Financial Ombudsman Service usually involve an inaccurate answer to one or more of those questions. Nondisclosure thus has come to assume a residual function. Below we consider whether it should still apply to consumer insurance. We therefore start by setting out the law of misrepresentation, before considering the law of nondisclosure. We begin by outlining the rules relating to misrepresentation under insurance contract law and then consider misrepresentation under general contract law.

MISREPRESENTATION IN INSURANCE CONTRACT LAW

The Obligation not to Misrepresent Material Facts

A. an aspect of the common law duty of utmost good faith, the potential parties to a policy of insurance are under an obligation not to misrepresent facts that are material to the insurer's decision whether or not to accept the risk. Above, we point out that this obligation, whilst reciprocal, lies more heavily on the applicant for insurance. This emphasis is reflected in section 20(1) of the MIA 1906 which deals only with the obligation of applicants: Every material representation made by the assured or his agent to the insurer during the negotiations for the contract, and before the contract is concluded, must be true. If it be untrue the insurer may avoid the contract.

THE TEST OF MATERIALITY

It might be thought that when a proposal form asks a question, the answer would always be material and, if it were inaccurate, would amount to a misrepresentation. However this is often not so. Many questions are asked in rather general terms and it is difficult to know the full extent of what is wanted. For example, an insured who is asked if they have had medical tests for illness may not interpret this as referring to routine tests (e.g. blood pressure checks) or even to nonroutine tests that were completely negative. The answer may be inaccurate or incomplete, but if the insurer is to have a remedy for misrepresentation the inaccuracy or incompleteness must also be material. The test of materiality is set out in Section 20(2) of the MIA 1906: A representation is material which would influence the judgment of a prudent insurer in fixing the premium, or determining whether he will take the risk.

Until 1994, there were two further vital questions relating to the interpretation of the section 20(2) test:

(1) Does "would influence the judgment" require that the influence would be decisive? There are no doubt many matters of which an insurer would wish to be aware. Some will be decisive in the decisionmaking process for example, a prior conviction for insurance fraud may of itself lead an insurer to decline an application. Others will not be decisive but may, taken with other factors, affect an insurer's assessment of the risk.

(2) When is the remedy of avoidance available? In particular, can an insurer avoid a policy if it was not induced to enter into it by the misrepresentation?

For English law, these questions were answered in the landmark case of *Pan Atlantic Insurance Co Ltd v Pine Top Insurance Co Ltd. 9* The House of Lords decided that:

(1) A material circumstance is one that would have an effect on the mind of the prudent insurer in assessing the risk and it is not necessary that it would have a decisive effect on the insurer's acceptance of the risk or on the amount of premium charged.

(2) Before an insurer may avoid a contract for misrepresentation of a material circumstance it has to show that it was induced by the misrepresentation to enter into the policy on the relevant terms.

In Scots law, the *Pan Atlantic* test of materiality applies other than for life insurance. Materiality in the case of life assurance is judged by the "reasonable assured" test, set out in *Life Association of Scotland v Foster*. Lord President Inglis described the insured's duty as follows:

His duty is carefully and diligently to review all the facts known to himself bearing on the risk proposed to the insurers, and to state every circumstance which any reasonable man might suppose could in any way influence the insurers in considering and deciding whether they will enter into the contract.

In *Cuthbertson v Friends' Provident Life Office,* Lord Eassie observed that the *Foster* test has two elements:

(1) For any fact to be material, it must be material in the view of the reasonable underwriter " If the fact were regarded by such an underwriter as of no significance, *cadit quaestio 14.*"

(2) Additionally, the insurer must show that either:

(a) "The proposer appreciated that the fact in question would have had that significance", or, assuming that the proposer did not have that appreciation,

(b) "A reasonable person making the proposal and possessed with the factual knowledge possessed by the actual proposer would think that fact to be material to the insurer".

Given that the obligation lies primarily on the proposer, it seems preferable to look at the issue from the point of view of a reasonable person making the proposal.

UNUSUAL VIEWS, NICHE MARKETS AND AFFINITY SCHEMES

There is an aspect of both the *Pan Atlantic* and the *Cuthbertson* tests which is uncertain and which may operate against the interests of the insurer. Where an insurer asks a clear question it seems reasonable that it should expect the prospective policyholder to take adequate care to answer correctly, and that a suitable remedy should be available where there is a failure to do so. However, the first limbs of the *Pan Atlantic* and *Cuthbertson* tests are objective. What happens, therefore, when the clear question relates to a matter material to this particular insurer but which would be irrelevant to any other insurer?

An underwriter may, for example, take a different attitude to the rest of the market in assessing a particular type of risk based on experience, difference of opinion or a desire to carve out a niche market. The issue may also arise with affinity schemes. An insurer may, for example, offer a special deal on household insurance to members of a particular union. For the rest of the market, membership of that union is irrelevant to the assessment of the risk. However the insurer in question will ask a specific question which will determine whether wider cover and a lower premium are granted.

If a wrong answer is given by an applicant for insurance, and no fraud is involved, will the insurer have a remedy? The question relates to facts that are not material under the first limbs of the *Pan Atlantic* and *Cuthbertson* tests or under section 20(2) of the Marine Insurance Act 1906. If the courts were to apply these tests strictly, there is no actionable misrepresentation even though the wrong answer may induce the contract.

A partial answer may be that it will be necessary to consider some characteristics of the actual insurer to establish what a reasonably prudent insurer would regard as material:

> For example, in the case of a proposed motor insurance, it would surely be appropriate to ask what the reasonably prudent motor insurer would regard as material. It struck me that there may be other characteristics of the particular insurer which might be relevant. So here, it seems to me that it might be relevant to ask whether a speeding conviction

would be material to the reasonably prudent insurer with a 'points' system of underwriting.

Belief or Fact?

A statement of opinion or belief is not in itself a statement of fact. However, the person expressing the opinion or belief impliedly represents that they genuinely believe it to be true. If they express it dishonestly, they therefore make a fraudulent misrepresentation. Section 20(3) of the MIA 1906 provides: A representation may be either a representation as to a matter of fact, or as to a matter of expectation or belief.

In general contract law the courts have often held that there is not only a representation that the opinion or belief is honestly held but also that it is based on reasonable grounds. 16 Insurance law differs in that there is no representation that there are reasonable grounds for the opinion or belief. The absence of this requirement derives from section 20(5) of the MIA 1906:

A representation as to a matter of expectation or belief is true if it be made in good faith.

An illustration of this principle is to be found in *Economides v Commercial Union Assurance Co.* A 21 year old man undervalued the contents of his flat after his parents moved in with him. As his statements on this issue were found to be a matter of opinion rather than fact, it was sufficient that they were held in good faith. It was not necessary that they should be based on reasonable grounds. The remedies for misrepresentation under the MIA 1906

Under the MIA 1906 the remedy for misrepresentation is avoidance. An insurer may avoid a policy regardless of whether the misrepresentation by the consumer was fraudulent, negligent or entirely innocent. Avoidance normally requires restitution: the parties must be restored to the positions they were in prior to the contract being made. This has two important elements:

(1) The insurer may reject any claim that has been made, and recover any claims payments already made.

(2) In most cases, the policyholder may demand the return of the premium paid.

There is an exception to (2) in the case of fraudulent misrepresentation. For marine insurance the matter is dealt with by section 84(3)(a) of the MIA 1906, which states:

Where the policy is void, or is avoided by the insurer as from the commencement of the risk, the premium is returnable, provided that there has been no fraud or illegality on the part of the assured...

For nonmarine insurance, the point is not wholly clear, and depends on general principles of contract law.

Misrepresentation in General Contract Law

The insurer's rights under the MIA 1906 are, at least in principle, supplemented by and qualified by the general law of misrepresentation. The law in this area is particularly complex, and is set in more detail. Here we deal only with three points: the availability of damages restrictions on the right to avoid (or "rescind") a contract that has been entered as the result of a misrepresentation~ and whether the general law provides the only remedy for misrepresentations that are not material to the risk.

The Right to Damages

In both jurisdictions the victim of a fraudulent misrepresentation is entitled to claim damages. A misrepresentor commits the tort of deceit in English law or entitles the other party to reparation in Scots law if they make a material statement (which causes loss) that they know is not true, or if they know the statement may or may not be true and make it nonetheless. In each jurisdiction there is now also, in effect, liability in damages created by statute for negligent misrepresentation by one of the parties to the contract.

In England and Wales, a party who makes a nonfraudulent misrepresentation will nonetheless be liable in damages "as if he were fraudulent" unless they prove that they had reasonable ground to believe, and did believe up to the time the contract was made, that the facts represented were true. In Scotland, the statute appears to create liability for negligent misrepresentation without resorting to the English "fiction of fraud".

In principle, therefore, an insurer that has suffered a loss as the result of a fraudulent or negligent misrepresentation can recover damages. However a leading authority on English insurance writes that there are no known cases in which an insurer has claimed damages from an insured. This is perhaps not surprising, even in cases of fraud. The main potential loss to the insurer will normally be prevented by avoidance of the policy, and if there has been fraud the insurer's right to retain the premium will probably cancel out any further loss.

Restrictions on the Right to Rescind

In England and Wales, section 2(2) of the Misrepresentation Act 1967 gives the court a discretion to refuse to permit rescission for nonfraudulent misrepresentation. It must then award damages in lieu of rescission. In principle this might be applied to an insurance case, but it has been held that it should not normally be applied to commercial insurance. It is unclear whether it might apply to consumer cases, and we have not found a case in which the point has been taken.

Misrepresentations that are not Relevant to the Risk

There has been a recent suggestion without a decision being reached that a fact is not material unless it goes to the risk insured: The nonpayment of premium is either material on its own or not, and since it seems to go to the owner's credit risk, and not to the risk insured, I would have thought it was not material.

However, there is conflicting earlier authority, and it is difficult to reconcile the suggestion with the clear wording of section 20(2) of the MIA 1906. The Act applies to failures to disclose or misrepresentations of facts that are material. What is material is defined in terms not as to what is relevant to the risk but what "would influence the judgment of a prudent insurer in fixing the premium, or determining whether he will take the risk." A failure to disclose or a misrepresentation about the insured's credit record is within the section if it would influence a reasonable insurer's decision whether or not to accept the risk.

NONDISCLOSURE

As an aspect of the common law duty of utmost good faith, the potential parties to a policy of insurance are under an obligation to disclose all material facts, subject to the exceptions discussed below. There is no obligation in insurance contract law for insurers to ask any questions at all at the time of an application or renewal.

It may come as a surprise to many policyholders – particularly consumers that they are expected to disclose information about which they have not been asked. In our Scoping Paper we quoted Professor Malcolm Clarke's criticism of the current position:

Applicants in England may complete the form with scrupulous care, but still find that there was something else material to prudent insurers which, apparently, the particular insurer did not think to ask about but which, nonetheless, the applicant was expected to think of and disclose.

The Obligation to Disclose Material Facts

Section 18(1) of the MIA 1906 expresses the obligation on applicants in the following terms:

Subject to the provisions of this section, the assured must disclose to the insurer, before the contract is concluded, every material circumstance which is known to the assured, and the assured is deemed to know every circumstance which, in the ordinary course of business, ought to be known by him. If the assured fails to make such disclosure, the insurer may avoid the contract.

It is only business policyholders who are deemed to know every circumstance which in the ordinary course of business ought to be known by them. We discuss this point further in Part 6.

The Test of Materiality

The test of materiality is set out in Section 18(2) of the MIA 1906: Every circumstance is material which would influence the judgment of a prudent insurer in fixing the premium, or determining whether he will take the risk.

This is the same test as found in Section 20(2) of the MIA 1906, and the points made earlier in relation to misrepresentation are therefore applicable.

Exceptions

There are four categories of exception to the general duty of disclosure:

(1) Facts which reduce the risk. It may not, of course, always be clearcut whether a risk is reduced. A sprinkler system, for example, may reduce losses by

fire. However, false activation of the system may cause damage which would otherwise not have occurred.

(2) Facts which the insurer knows or is presumed to know.

(3) Facts which are common knowledge.

(4) Facts of which the insurer has waived disclosure.

Remedies

Avoidance

As with misrepresentation, the remedy for nondisclosure is that the insurer may avoid the contract.

Damages

A breach of the duty of good faith does not of itself give rise to a right to damages. In *Banque Keyser v Skandia,* Steyn J suggested that such a right existed: Once it is accepted that the principle of the utmost good faith imposes meaningful reciprocal duties, owed to the insurers and vice versa, it seems anomalous that there should be no claim for damages for breach of those duties in a case where that is the only remedy. However, this suggestion was rejected when the case proceeded to the Court of Appeal. Amongst five reasons given was the fact that damages are simply not mentioned in the sections of the MIA 1906 that deal with the obligation of good faith:

> We think the clear inference from the Act of 1906 is that Parliament did not contemplate that a breach of the obligation would give rise to a claim for damages in the case of such contracts. Otherwise it would surely have said so. It is not suggested that a remedy is available in the case of nonmarine policies which would not be available in the case of marine policies.

Despite some contrary suggestions, it seems to be accepted as settled law in England and Wales that even deliberate nondisclosure does not give rise to liability in damages, as deceit or fraud requires a positive misrepresentation.

RENEWALS

With the exception of some types of life insurance, most insurance policies have a fixed term. Typically this is one year, at the end of which the policy falls due for renewal. Although the process is referred to as "renewal" the legal position is clear a new contract is formed. The law of misrepresentation and nondisclosure therefore applies to renewals in the same way as it applies to fresh applications for insurance.

At renewal, however, there may be an additional potential pitfall for a policyholder. Rather than or in addition to specific questions, an insurer may simply ask whether there has been any change in material circumstances. To be certain of answering this question accurately, a policyholder should review all the information previously submitted to the insurer. Unfortunately the policyholder will not usually have been given a copy of the original proposal form, and in many cases will not have retained copies of information submitted at subsequent renewals.

BASIS OF THE CONTRACT CLAUSES

A basis of the contract clause is a legal device used to turn representations into warranties. Typically, applicants are asked to sign a proposal form containing a clause declaring that they warrant the accuracy of all the answers they have given. The clause usually states that the answers "form the basis" of the contract. Such clauses elevate the answers in proposal forms to contractual warranties, even if the terms are not to be found in the contract itself. This means that in effect an insurer may avoid liability for an inaccurate representation, even if it was not material. For example, in *Dawsons Ltd v Bonnin*, the insured was asked where their lorry was garaged. They inadvertently gave the firm's place of business in central Glasgow, though the lorry was usually kept in the outskirts. This did not increase the risk, and arguably decreased it. However, when the lorry was destroyed by fire, the insurers were allowed to treat the policy as terminated by the breach of warranty, even though the misrepresentation was immaterial.

Although the effect of basis of the contract clauses has been confirmed as recently as 1996, there has been widespread criticism of their use. In 1997, the National Consumer Council described them as "completely unfair". We understand that they have been outlawed in Australia and New Zealand. For example, section 24 of the Australian Insurance Contracts Act 1984 provides that a statement by the insured about the existence of a current state of affairs should take effect only as a representation, not as a warranty. A provision along similar lines may be needed to prevent evasion of our other proposals. Our present view is that an insurer should not be able to rely on a simple basis of the contract clause to give it rights that it would not have under the law of misrepresentation or nondisclosure.

We note with interest that the Statement of General Insurance Practice effectively prohibited the use of basis of the contract clauses in consumer insurances. However, we intend to address the matter more fully in our second issues paper, which will be on warranties.

PREVIOUS REPORTS, SELFREGULATION AND STATUTORY REGULATION

In this Part we provide an overview of some of the more important measures of selfregulation and statutory regulation introduced in recent years. We do so because we believe that some knowledge of these developments is vital to understanding the current position of consumers, which we discuss later. Given this limited purpose we have not attempted to provide a full history, and indeed we have omitted some measures altogether.

This is also a convenient point to consider some of the previous reports which called for reform, and to outline the recommendations they have made in respect of consumers and businesses.

ENGLISH LAW REFORM COMMITTEE REPORT 1957

Insurance contract law was considered by the Law Reform Committee in 1957. The Committee did not make formal recommendations, but suggested three reforming provisions it felt could be enacted without legal difficulties:

(1) For the purposes of a contract of insurance no fact should be deemed material unless it would have been considered material by a reasonable insured.

(2) An insurer should not be able to rely on misrepresentation if the insured could prove that the statement was true to the best of the insured's knowledge and belief.

(3) An intermediary who arranged a contract of insurance should be deemed for the purposes of the formation of the contract, to be the agent of the insurer. Consequently anything disclosed to the intermediary would be deemed disclosed to the insurer.

These suggestions were not implemented.

A similar report by the Law Reform Committee for Scotland made no proposals for reform, concluding that there was "...no demand in Scotland for any alteration in the law with regard to the subject of our remit".

THE STATEMENTS OF PRACTICE 1977

In 1977 the British Insurance Association (predecessor to the ABI) and Lloyd's issued a Statement of General Insurance Practice ("SGIP"). This was followed later in the same year by a Statement of LongTerm Insurance Practice ("SLIP") issued by the Life Offices' Association (now part of the ABI) and the Associated Scottish Life Offices.

It appears that these Statements were introduced as part of an agreement with the Government, under which insurance contracts were exempted from key provisions of the Unfair Contract Terms Act 1977. 5 We are told that the title "Statement" was chosen in preference to "Code" to make it clear that in the industry's view the provisions merely confirmed current practice.

It was intended that the Statements would address some of the harsher aspects of the law for consumers. Both Statements required proposal forms to contain warnings regarding the duty of disclosure and the consequences of any breach. In addition, insurers were required to ask clear questions about matters which were generally found to be material.

The Statements did not directly change the test of materiality. Nor did they explicitly refer to avoidance. They did, however, restrict the right of an insurer to repudiate liability for a claim – and such repudiation could only take place after the policy had been avoided. The Statements did not address the situation where no claim had been made. Whilst many allegations of misrepresentation or nondisclosure are undoubtedly raised after a claim, these issues can arise in other circumstances.

SGIP provided that in cases of fraud, deception or negligence, an insurer's right to repudiate a claim remained unchanged. Otherwise presumably in cases where a misrepresentation or nondisclosure was innocent insurers should not: Unreasonably repudiate liability to indemnify a policyholder:on the grounds of nondisclosure or misrepresentation of a material fact where knowledge of the fact would not materially have influenced the insurer's judgment in the acceptance or assessment of the insurance.

This effectively anticipated the *Pan Atlantic* decision by requiring actual inducement.

SLIP was less clear: An insurer will not unreasonably reject a claim. (However, fraud or deception will, and negligence or nondisclosure or misrepresentation of a material fact may, result in adjustment or constitute grounds for rejection). In particular, an insurer will not reject a claim on grounds of nondisclosure or misrepresentation of a matter that was outside the knowledge of the proposer.

The word "or" between negligence and nondisclosure suggests that these are separate grounds for rejection of a claim. If this is correct, the only obligation on the insurer in respect of misrepresentation or nondisclosure is not to "unreasonably" reject a claim.

The weak nature of the protections offered by the Statements led one academic to describe them as "a rather pointless exercise".

Detailed criticisms of the Statements were also made in the English Law Commission's Report of 1980.

ENGLISH LAW COMMISSION REPORT 1980

In 1975, a draft European Directive called for the harmonisation of the essential provisions of insurance contract law. By 1978 there was a separate draft Directive modelled on French law and aimed at achieving a measure of harmonisation. In 1978, against this background, the Lord Chancellor referred insurance contract law to the Commission.

The Central Problem

The report concluded that the current duty of disclosure is far too stringent. It argued that a duty of disclosure based on what a "prudent insurer" thinks is material is inherently unreasonable: It requires every insured to disclose any fact which a prudent insurer would consider to be material, and entitles the insurer to repudiate the policy and to reject any claim in the event of any breach of this duty. However, an honest and reasonable insured may be quite unaware of the existence and extent of this duty, and even if he is aware of it, he may have great difficulty in forming any view as to what facts a prudent insurer would consider to be material."

As a result, a policyholder may act honestly and reasonably and still find that the insurer is entitled to avoid the policy. Furthermore, the duty of disclosure can operate as a trap in relation to proposal and renewal forms. A reasonable insured may think that it is sufficient to answer the questions presented, and find that they are later deprived of the cover they thought they had bought.

Voluntary Measures Unsatisfactory

The insurance industry did not attempt to defend the law in its present form. Instead, they argued that any faults had been cured through the 1977 Statements of Practice. However, the Law Commission thought that the statements "are themselves evidence that the law is unsatisfactory and needs to be changed".

It gave three reasons:

(1) The Statements left insurers as the sole judge of whether rejection of a claim was reasonable.

(2) The Statements did not have the force of law and, indeed, the liquidator of an insurance company would be bound to disregard them.

(3) The Statements were restricted to policyholders effecting policies in their private capacity but the mischiefs in the law also affected businesses.

The Commission was particularly scathing about the suggestion that insurers should have discretion "to repudiate a policy on technical grounds if they suspect fraud but are unable to prove it". This placed insurers in the position of judge in their own cause.

Modifying the Duty of Disclosure

The Commission considered that the duty of disclosure should be modified rather than abolished. It thought that insurers still relied on information volunteered by policyholders. Without it, insurers would be less able to differentiate between good and bad quality risks, leading to higher premiums for honest and reasonable policyholders.

This approach applied to both consumers and businesses. The Commission thought that abolition would enable "sharp practice" by consumers. It would also hamper the granting of temporary cover prior to a proposal form being completed. Indeed, any division between consumers and business was thought by the Commission to be artificial~ it felt the dividing line should really be between "professionals" and "nonprofessionals".

Special rules for consumers would lead to complex law, as there would then be three categories:

(1) Consumers.

(2) Businesses.

(3) Marine, Aviation and Transport risks.

So far as businesses were concerned, most other systems of law imposed such a duty and abolition might cause the British insurance industry to lose international competitiveness. Instead, the Commission attempted to draw a better balance between the interests of the insurer and those of the policyholder.

A Reasonable Insured Test

The Commission recommended that an applicant for insurance should only be required to disclose those facts that a reasonable person in the position of the applicant would disclose. Thus an applicant for insurance would be obliged to disclose a fact only if:

(1) It is material in the sense that it would influence a prudent insurer in deciding whether to offer cover against the proposed risk and, if so, at what premium and on what terms~ and

(2) It is either known to the applicant or it is one which the applicant can be assumed to know. For this purpose the applicant should be assumed to know a material fact if it would have been ascertainable by reasonable enquiry and if a reasonable person applying for the insurance in question would have ascertained it~ and

(3) It is one which a reasonable person in the position of the applicant would disclose to the insurer, having regard to the nature and extent of the insurance cover which is sought and the circumstances in which it is sought.

The final limb allows the court to make a distinction between, say, a small business and a large business with inhouse insurance expertise. However, it was not intended that an individual's personal characteristics would be considered.

Regard should be had to the nature and extent of the insurance cover sought. A reasonable person might not disclose facts relevant to health when applying for a household policy, and a lesser degree of disclosure might be expected from those applying for mere temporary cover. The circumstances in which cover is sought should be considered. An application by telephone might be treated differently to an application made on paper.

Only Reasonable Enquiries

It was felt that a policyholder should be required to make reasonable enquiries, but not to undertake elaborate investigations. The Commission recommended that even if an answer on a proposal form proved to be inaccurate, a policyholder should be regarded as having met the duty of disclosure if two conditions were satisfied:

(1) The policyholder, before answering, had carried out enquiries that were reasonable having regard to the subject matter of the question and the nature and extent of the cover sought.

(2) The answer was correct to the policyholder's best knowledge and belief. In such circumstances, it was also recommended that the insurer should not be entitled to pursue an alternative remedy for misrepresentation.

Proposal and Renewal Forms

The Commission recommended that proposal forms should contain clear, explicit and prominent warnings about the standard of answers required, the duty to volunteer information and the consequences of failing to meet these obligations.

A copy of the completed proposal form should be provided to a policyholder after completion or as soon after as is reasonably practicable.

In the event of a failure to meet these requirements, an insurer would be unable to rely on any nondisclosure by the policyholder — subject to the court having a discretion to allow the insurer to rely on the nondisclosure if the failure caused no prejudice to the policyholder.

The Commission further recommended that if a policy had been initiated by the completion of a proposal form the insurer should only have a remedy for nondisclosure at renewal if it had taken the following steps:

(1) Supplied the policyholder with copies of any information that the policyholder had previously submitted to the insurer.

(2) Warned the policyholder of the importance of retaining such copies.

(3) Warned the policyholder of the duty to volunteer information and the consequences of failing to meet this obligation.

For policies not initiated by proposal form, only the third step was required.

Antiavoidance

The Commission recommended measures to prevent insurers from avoiding the reforms.

First, it thought that where a policyholder's failure to provide an insurer with information amounts to both a nondisclosure and a nonfraudulent misrepresentation, an insurer's rights would be limited to those — if any — available for nondisclosure.

Secondly, it recommended measures to curb the use of "basis of the contract" clauses. The Commission recommended that such clauses should be ineffective insofar as they seek to create warranties as to past or present fact.

Rejected Options

The English Law Commission specifically rejected two further options for reform.

No Requirement for a Causal Link

The Commission rejected the idea that the insurer would be required to show a link between a nondisclosure and any loss that had occurred. It argued that an insurer assesses a risk at a fixed point the time at which an application for insurance is considered. A nondisclosure may cause it to offer cover which it would not otherwise have granted, or where a different premium or different terms would have been applied. It would be wrong to hold an insurer to such a contract. Furthermore, where the nondisclosure relates to moral hazard, such as the applicant's claims record or criminal convictions, it would be rare that a link can be shown with any loss that occurs. It seems unfair that the insurer has no remedy when the applicant has acted unreasonably.

The "all or nothing" Rule Maintained

The Commission concluded that there should not be a remedy based on the proportionality principle. It specifically rejected the idea that claims should be reduced to reflect the ratio between the premium paid and the premium that should have been paid. In many cases it would be difficult to establish what premium should have been charged. Furthermore, the insurer may not necessarily have charged a higher premium: it may have declined the risk altogether or imposed additional warranties, exclusion clauses, or excesses. In such cases a reduction in the claim paid would become arbitrary.

THE INSURANCE OMBUDSMAN BUREAU 1981

The Insurance Ombudsman Bureau ("IOB") was the first privatesector ombudsman scheme in the UK, and the first complaintshandling service formally to use the title "ombudsman". It was established on a voluntary basis by three insurers and commenced operations in March 1981.

The IOB investigated complaints against insurers and was able to make awards which, if accepted by the complainant, were binding on an insurer to a limit of £100,000. Until 1994, it could consider complaints relating to general or life insurance.

The ombudsman concept met with enthusiasm from the public. Further insurers joined until almost all were members.

THE STATEMENTS OF PRACTICE 1986

The 1980 report was never implemented. Instead, the industry reached agreement with the Government that the Statements of Practice would be strengthened in place of law reform.

On 31 October 1980 the Department of Trade and Industry circulated a consultation paper seeking views on the English Law Commission's 1980 report. The responses indicated a division of opinion between consumers and others who wished to see reform, and insurers who argued that there was no need for radical or urgent change.

In 1984 the DTI put forward a Bill based on the 1980 report but limited to consumers. However, this was subsequently abandoned and on 20 December 1984 the Secretary of State made the following announcement: I am embarking on discussions with the insurance industry to see whether changes to their statements of insurance practice can be made to deal with problems in those areas. I shall review whether legislation is appropriate and feasible in the light of whatever changes may be agreed.

On 21 February 1986, the Secretary of State confirmed that the DTI had accepted changes in the Statements as an alternative to law reform: The insurers have informed me that they are willing to strengthen the nonlife and longterm statements of insurance practice on certain aspects proposed by the Department.... I am well aware of the arguments, advanced amongst others by the representatives of consumers, in favour of legislation on nondisclosure and breach of warranty. But I consider that on balance the case for legislation is outweighed by the advantages of selfregulation so long as this is effective.

The 1986 version of SGIP remained in force until 14 January 2005. It was then withdrawn with the introduction of statutory conduct of business regulation for general insurance. However, it continues to be taken into account by the Financial Ombudsman Service as an indicator of good practice.

3

FINANCIAL SERVICES ACT 1986

LAUTRO AND FIMBRA

Regulation of the conduct of investment business was introduced in 1988 under the Financial Services Act 1986. It was a twotier system, with a statutory regulator the Securities and Investments Board overseeing selfregulating organisations and recognised professional bodies. The two selfregulating organisations for insurance were the Life Assurance and Unit Trust Regulatory Organisation ("LAUTRO") and the Financial Intermediaries, Managers and Brokers Association ("FIMBRA"). LAUTRO appointed IOB to act as its primary complaintshandling mechanism. For most of the time FIMBRA operated, it offered an arbitration scheme.

PIA

In 1994 LAUTRO and FIMBRA were replaced by a single selfregulating organisation the Personal Investment Authority ("PIA"). The PIA established its own Ombudsman, leading the IOB to lose jurisdiction over life insurance.

NATIONAL CONSUMER COUNCIL REPORT 1997

In 1997 the National Consumer Council ("NCC") published a report written by Professor John Birds, then of Sheffield University, which considered the impact of insurance law on consumers:

Almost every household in the country regularly buys personal insurance of one kind and another, to safeguard the value of their personal belongings, home, income, health, travel and so on, in case of crime, accident or other disaster. And every time they buy – or renew – a policy, the transaction is governed by law that has remained largely unchanged for hundreds of years. Large parts of that law, it is widely acknowledged, are heavily biased against the interests of consumers.

The NCC took into account the 1986 Statements of Practice but concluded that there were still areas "where consumers are manifestly still at risk". It recommended reform in a range of areas: We conclude that the only effective solution to some of the serious problems encountered by consumers when it comes to buying personal insurance is legislative reform.

With regard to misrepresentation and nondisclosure the NCC made a series of recommendations.

The Test of Materiality

The NCC recommended that a consumer should be required to disclose those facts within the consumer's knowledge which either the consumer knows to be relevant to the insurer's decision or which a reasonable person in the circumstances could be expected to know to be relevant.

It also recommended that an untrue statement should not be treated as a misrepresentation if the applicant honestly believed it to be true.

Remedies

The NCC recommended that avoidance should continue to be available as a remedy for fraudulent misrepresentation or nondisclosure. For other cases, the rights of the insurer would depend on the action the insurer would have taken had it known of the true facts:

(1) If the insurer would have declined to offer cover, it should be entitled to avoid the policy.

(2) If the insurer would have offered cover, it should retain liability under the policy but should be entitled to deduct the extra premium it would have charged had there been no nondisclosure or misrepresentation.

GENERAL INSURANCE STANDARDS COUNCIL

In July 2000, a voluntary regulator was established for general insurance. Membership was open to insurers and intermediaries. Regulation was based on two codes the GISC Private Customer Code for consumer insurances and the GISC Commercial Code for business insurances.

THE PAT SAXTON MEMORIAL LECTURE 2001

In March 2001 Lord Justice Longmore gave the Pat Saxton Memorial Lecture. He took the opportunity to propose a new Insurance Contracts Act, dealing with, amongst other issues, misrepresentation and nondisclosure. He made a number of suggestions for reform.

Test of Materiality

Lord Justice Longmore identified a number of possible formulations for the test of materiality, and expressed support for a formulation that depends on what the reasonable insured would think was material. He has since said judicially: Is it not time that the law was changed at least to the extent that an insured's disclosure obligation should be to disclose matters which the insured knows are relevant to the insurer's decision to accept the risk or which a reasonable assured could be expected to know are relevant to that decision.

Remedies

He suggested that the courts might be given a discretion to adjust the respective responsibilities of insured and insurer instead of allowing avoidance:

It would, of course, lead to some uncertainty but that, after all, was a reason against the introduction of the concept of contributory negligence which, in the event, is a concept that has worn the test of time very well. In these days when the incidence of costs in litigation may depend on well or ill informed guesses made by the litigant, at the time they are obliged to serve pre action protocols, uncertainty is endemic, yet the court, and litigants, are quite good at getting used to it. Moreover, the Insurance Ombudsman Bureau apparently uses its discretion on occasion to apportion the loss and appears to have no difficulty with the concept.

THE FINANCIAL SERVICES AND MARKETS ACT 2000

COB

One of the earliest acts of the Labour government formed in May 1997 was an announcement that it intended to introduce statutory regulation for the financial services industry with a single regulator – the Financial Services Authority ("FSA"). This new system was introduced in 2001 under the Financial Services and Markets Act 2000 ("FiSMA")

The FSA sets out its Rules for regulated firms in its Handbook. With effect from 1 December 2001 the FSA took responsibility for conduct of business regulation of investment insurance. The relevant Rules are to be found in the Conduct of Business ("COB") sourcebook. On 13 July 2005, the FSA announced that it would be simplifying the COB regime to make it "easier to understand, comply with, enforce and amend" 22. It is anticipated that a revised structure for the COB sourcebook will be introduced in November 2007 at the same time as the Markets in Financial Instruments Directive ("MiFID") is implemented.

Financial Ombudsman Service

When this new system was being designed, it was decided that there should be a single complaintshandling body — the Financial Ombudsman Service.

The Financial Ombudsman Service ("FOS") therefore replaced eight existing disputeresolution mechanisms, including the Insurance Ombudsman Bureau and the Personal Investment Authority Ombudsman. It was established under Part 16 and Schedule 17 of FiSMA. In addition, Rules relating to the FOS can be found in the *Dispute Resolution: Complaints* sourcebook ("DISP") within the FSA Handbook. Although the FOS has both a compulsory and a voluntary jurisdiction, it is the former that is of primary importance for current purposes.

Provided that certain preliminary conditions are met, the FOS can consider complaints against insurers and intermediaries. Both complainant and the complaint must be within the scope of the scheme, and the complaint must be brought within the relevant time limits and not subject to dismissal without consideration of its merits. Complaints may be referred to the FOS by private individuals, and by sole traders and small businesses with a turnover of less than £1 million.

Chapter 1 of DISP contains rules relating to the internal handling of complaints by firms: The purpose of this chapter is to set out the rules relating to the internal handling of complaints by firms, including the procedures which a firm must put in place~ the time limits within which a firm must deal with a complaint~ the referral of complaints, the records of a complaint which a firm must make and retain and the requirements on a firm to report information about complaints to the FSA. This is to ensure that complaints are handled fairly, effectively and promptly, and resolved at the earliest possible opportunity, minimising the number of unresolved complaints which need to be referred to the Financial Ombudsman Service.

BRITISH INSURANCE LAW ASSOCIATION REPORT 2002

In 2002 the British Insurance Law Association ("BILA") submitted a report to the English Law Commission in which it recommended reform of various aspects of insurance contract law. This report is of particular interest in that it was drafted by a subcommittee whose members included insurance practitioners as well as academics and lawyers. The introduction to the report indicated clearly that the state of the law was now a matter of concern to the market:

> This SubCommittee was formed in January 2001 to examine areas of insurance law causing concern in the insurance market and in insurance disputes, and to make recommendations to the Law Commission as to the desirability of drafting a new Insurance Contracts Act in respect of Marine and NonMarine Insurance and/or other reforms to current legislation.

BILA made recommendations affecting both the test of materiality and the remedies available to insurers.

The Test of Materiality

BILA recommended that the test of materiality should be amended so that an applicant for insurance would be obliged to disclose those matters which a reasonable insured would have considered material to a prudent insurer.

Remedies

BILA recommended that avoidance should continue to be available as a remedy for fraudulent or reckless misrepresentation or nondisclosure. In addition, the insurer would have the right to retain the premium paid.

Where a misrepresentation was innocent or negligent, BILA recommended a response depending on the action an insurer would have taken had it known of the true facts:

(1) If the insurer would have declined to offer cover, it could avoid the policy but would be obliged to return the premium.

(2) If the insurer would have offered cover on different terms, it could not avoid the policy but:

   (a) would not be liable for any loss proximately caused by the fact that was misrepresented or not disclosed, and

   (b) could vary its liability to reflect any variation in premium deductible or excess that would have been imposed had it known of the true facts.

ICOB 2005

On 14 January 2005, the FSA took over responsibility for conduct of business regulation of general insurance. The Rules for "pure protection insurance" are contained in the Insurance Conduct of Business ("ICOB") sourcebook. On the same date, the GISC was closed and SGIP was withdrawn.

The FSA is currently conducting a postimplementation effectiveness review of ICOB. Its objectives have been described by Mr Dan Waters, Director of Retail Policy at the FSA in the following terms: Effectiveness reviews are part of the FSA's approach seeking to ensure that its interventions in the market make a real and beneficial difference in practice. We are seeking to introduce more principlesbased regulation and simplification across the FSA Handbook as a whole in the context of our Better Regulation agenda. And the GI effectiveness review presents a good and timely opportunity to look at ICOB in fine detail from the viewpoint of restricting prescription to the point where it is only demonstrably necessary to meet our consumer protection objective.

A report from the FSA is anticipated in the first quarter of 2007.

APPLICATION FORM DESIGN – GUIDANCE FROM THE ABI 2006

In February 2006, the ABI issued guidance to its members on the design and wording of proposal forms for life and health insurance. This guidance, entitled *Application Form Design for Life and Health Protection Insurances* ("AFD") was aimed at ensuring that all relevant information is disclosed at the application stage: Although not all nondisclosure arises because of faults in proposal forms, insurers should do as much as they can to ensure that the questions they ask are clear and unambiguous. Doing so assists the applicant in their understanding of what is being asked of them. Thus when completing a proposal form, they should have confidence they are giving all the necessary correct and relevant information. This will also reduce the burden on salespersons in explaining or interpreting how questions should be responded to.

The AFD has provisions relating to some of the problems that we identify in Part 6. It should, however, be noted at this stage that the AFD specifically states that its provisions are not binding on insurers except where they represent the law or the requirements of the Statements of Practice:

> In order to allow flexibility and to preserve competition between Insurers, the recommendations are not in any way prescriptive to ABI members, other than where existing legislation or Statements of Best Practice are applicable.

CONCLUSION

The General Law

Despite these various reports the law remains essentially unchanged and open to the same criticisms. The decision in *Pan Atlantic* made it clear that the insurer must show inducement, but the test of materiality is still based on whether a fact would have an effect on the mind of a prudent underwriter. Many policyholders will be unaware of the true extent of this onerous obligation, and few will be able to place themselves in the mind of a prudent underwriter. The weight of opinion in the reports we have discussed is clearly in favour of a move to a test based in some way on the reasonable insured, irrespective of whether the insured is a consumer or a business.

We need to review the law applying to insurance contracts of all types. However we need to distinguish between various types of policyholder.

Consumer Insurance

The result of the Statements of Practice, the COB and ICOB Rules and above all the FOS scheme mean that consumer insurance is subject to an additional set of rules that should go some way to improving the consumer's position so far as misrepresentation or nondisclosure is concerned. For this reason we deal with consumers and businesses separately. There are also reasons of substance that may make it sensible to treat consumer insurance separately.

Consumers might be thought to deserve more favourable treatment under the law than, say, large businesses because:

(1) Consumers will almost always contract on standard policy terms which they lack the bargaining power to alter.

(2) Consumers are unlikely to have access to the level of expert advice which will be available to large businesses whether inhouse or externally.

(3) Consumers are typically less able to understand the technicalities of insurance contract law particularly if it does not meet their reasonable expectations. Indeed, as the FOS has pointed out to us, consumers may not even be aware that there is an issue of law to be considered: There are two problems for consumers~ firstly they do not know that there are issues of insurance contract law and secondly, in the unlikely event that they do, they are less likely to understand them than a business advised by its broker or in house specialists.

This problem is compounded by the fact that expert broker or intermediary advice is hard to find for consumers and there is little understanding of the need to obtain this given the ignorance of the pitfalls in insurance contract law.

In this regard it is important to bear in mind that the reasonable expectations of the consumer may well be based upon their expectation of the law in relation to all, or nearly all, other consumer transactions that they may enter into. Applying for an insurance contract may be the only transaction to acquire goods or services that they enter into in any year in which they are expected in law to assume duties and responsibilities that are not known or explained to them and, where they are not required to seek expert assistance for their own benefit. Within consumer insurance we need to distinguish general insurance from longterm insurance. A special rule on longterm insurance needs to be considered.

Business Insurance

We consider in particular the extent to which the needs and circumstances of businesses genuinely differ from those of consumers. Our conclusion is that in some respects the differences are genuine, in others the two classes of policyholder should be treated in the same way.

We need to consider how any changes should affect reinsurance, and also whether marine, aviation and transport insurance need different treatment.

Small Businesses

We shall see that small businesses can also take advantage of the FOS scheme. At the end of Part 7 we consider whether they should be treated in the same way as other businesses, like consumers or in some other way.

4

CONSUMERS—THE CURRENT POSITION

INTRODUCTION

In this Part of the paper we look at how the strict legal rights of the consumer are supplemented by three measures the Statements of Practice issued by the Association of British Insurers ("ABI"), regulation by the Financial Services Authority ("FSA") and the dispute resolution service of the Financial Ombudsman Service ("FOS").

THE ABI STATEMENTS OF PRACTICE

The Statements address the problem of nondisclosure in three ways:

(1) It states that each proposal form should include a prominent warning, drawing attention to the consequences of failing to disclose material facts, and explaining that material facts are those which "an insurer would regard as likely to influence the acceptance and assessment of the proposal". Applicants must be warned that if they are in any doubt about whether facts are material, they should disclose them.

(2) SGIP states that "those matters which are generally found to be material should be the subject of clear

questions". However SGIP provides no sanction if this rule is not observed.

(3) Under SGIP, insurers undertake not to repudiate liability on grounds of nondisclosure of a material fact which a policyholder could not reasonably be expected to have disclosed. This effectively limits consumers' duty to volunteer information to facts which "a policyholder could reasonably be expected to disclose".

As far as misrepresentation is concerned, insurers undertake not to repudiate liability on grounds of misrepresentation unless it is a deliberate or negligent misrepresentation of a material fact.

We have found the Statements of Practice to be a useful indicator of what is accepted by the industry to be good practice. However, we believe that they are limited in their practical impact for the following reasons:

(1) Few consumers are likely to be aware of the existence of SGIP or SLIP.

(2) SGIP was withdrawn on 14 January 2005 (though it may still be applied by the FOS).

(3) The relevant provisions of SGIP and SLIP are limited in their effect and are not legally binding. They are enforced by the FOS but at that stage the question is whether they add anything to the general obligation on the FOS to reach a decision that is "fair and reasonable in all the circumstances".

THE FINANCIAL SERVICES AUTHORITY

There are several ways in which the FSA influences the approach taken by insurers to misrepresentation and nondisclosure. Most importantly, it has issued specific Rules in this area. In addition, it publishes high level principles and conducts initiatives such as *Treating Customers Fairly* ("TCF").

The Rules

It should be noted that where there are breaches of the Rules there are two potentially significant consequences under the Financial Services and Markets Act 2000. First an affected policyholder may bring a claim against a regulated firm for breach of statutory duty. 1 Secondly, the FSA may take disciplinary action against the firm and has the power, for example, to impose a fine. These are important provisions which will undoubtedly be invaluable in certain circumstances. However, for the following reasons we rather doubt that they are of significance in most daytoday cases:

(1) The specific Rules on misrepresentation and nondisclosure are largely based on the provisions of SGIP, and are subject to similar limitations on their effect.

(2) The vast majority of consumers will pursue disputes through the FOS rather than through the courts. 3 A right to bring an action for breach of statutory duty is unlikely to add anything to a consumer's right to receive a decision that is "fair and reasonable in all the circumstances". Serious disciplinary action is unlikely in what appear to be oneoff cases.

Relatively few consumers will complain to the FSA about matters of misrepresentation or nondisclosure.

We understand that those who do are most likely to be advised to pursue the matter through the FOS.

FSA Principles and Treating Customers Fairly

The FSA publishes eleven high level "Principles for Businesses", to be found in the PRIN Sourcebook of the

Handbook. These are part of a move away from prescriptive Rules to principlesbased regulation. Perhaps most importantly in the areas of misrepresentation and nondisclosure is Principle 6:

> A firm must pay due regard to the interests of its customers and treat them fairly.

This principle is being explored in the TCF initiative. We were interested to note, for example, that in the General Insurance Cluster report published in July 2006 the FSA highlighted disclosure issues as examples of both good and bad practice in claims handling:

> Good TCF examples we have seen include...
>
> 1. Firms stressing the importance of full disclosure by customers when completing a critical illness application. One firm included a case study for customers explaining the implications of nondisclosure.
> 2. A firm does full medical underwriting at the time of application to ensure both the firm and the customer are clear about the basis on which the cover is being provided.
>
> Examples of poor practice include...
>
> 3. Firms who provide little training to their distributors in issues such as application forms where technical medical questions can be asked and where the consequences of nondisclosure can be significant.

We believe that TCF is a valuable initiative which is influencing attitudes within the insurance industry. However, it was never intended to be a substitute for law reform and we do not think that it can be treated as such. The state of the law on misrepresentation and nondisclosure is such that swifter, more radical, and more consistent change is required.

THE FINANCIAL OMBUDSMAN SERVICE

Very few consumer insurance disputes are now considered by the courts. Instead, most complainants opt to use the service offered by the FOS. In its last year of operation, the FOS received 14,270 insurancerelated cases. This figure excludes a large number of complaints that the FOS received relating to investment contracts.

Research Project

When we commenced our review of insurance contract law we were struck by comments made by Lord Justice Longmore. He suggested that if we were to conduct such a review "the records of the Ombudsman Bureau will be an early port of call".

With the kind cooperation of the FOS we have therefore conducted a research project to assist our understanding of the experience of consumers. We reviewed around 200 cases that had been considered by the FOS and which involved allegations of misrepresentation or nondisclosure. Our findings will be published in a separate paper.

The sample included 12 small business cases. The FOS sees a relatively small number of such cases, possibly because insurers are under no obligation to bring the existence of the scheme to the attention of small business policyholders. We address the position of small businesses in Part 7 below.

From the work we have conducted we have no doubt that the FOS currently provides consumers with their best chance of achieving a fair result in cases where misrepresentation or nondisclosure is alleged. Its obligation to reach a decision that is "fair and reasonable in all the circumstances" enables it to set aside the strict law and to explore other solutions. We set out below in some detail the approach taken by the FOS and acknowledge here the significant influence its guidance has had on our thinking.

This is not to say that the FOS is a satisfactory alternative to law reform.

The FOS Approach to Complaints

The FOS seeks wherever possible to settle complaints by mediation. Should this prove impracticable, the case will be investigated and a view reached by an adjudicator. If either party remains dissatisfied, an appeal may be made to an Ombudsman. An Ombudsman has the power to make awards of up to £100,000 against an insurer, or instruct it to take specified steps, the cost of which should not exceed that limit.

Compulsory jurisdiction complaints are determined "by reference to what is, in the opinion of the ombudsman, fair and reasonable in all the circumstances of the case". 5 As explained above, this means that the FOS is not bound by the strict law. A case study illustrates the difference that this can make:

Case Study

Mr M made a claim under his household policy for possessions stolen after burglars gained access to his home by kicking in a panel in the back door. The insurer accepted the claim, and had the door replaced by one of its approved contractors. At the next renewal of the policy, Mr M completed a questionnaire for the insurer in which he confirmed that external doors had "a mortise deadlock and security bolts or a keyoperated locking system".

Shortly after the policy was renewed, Mr M suffered a second burglary when entry was again gained by kicking in a rear door panel. The insurer discovered that the door did not have security bolts or a keyoperated locking system. As a matter of law, the insurer was entitled to avoid the policy on the basis of the misrepresentation. It refused to pay Mr M's claim.

The FOS instructed the insurer to meet the claim. It gave three reasons:

1. Mr M had assumed the insurer would have had a door installed that met its own requirements. It was careless of him not to have checked this, but he had not deliberately or recklessly supplied an incorrect answer.
2. There was no link between the misrepresentation and the loss that occurred the burglars had entered the house by kicking in the door panel.
3. If Mr M had answered the question correctly, the firm would have allowed him time to change the locks. The burglary occurred within this timescale.

MISREPRESENTATION AND NONDISCLOSURE

As already indicated, the FOS enforces SLIP and takes note of SGIP. It also enforces COB and ICOB. However, to meet its obligation to reach a fair and reasonable decision in cases of misrepresentation and nondisclosure, the FOS has found it necessary to go significantly further than these measures.

The FOS approach to misrepresentation and nondisclosure is explained in a series of case studies and guidance notes in *Ombudsman News*. In *Ombudsman News Issue 46* the FOS indicated that in cases where misrepresentation or nondisclosure is alleged, it asks two questions:

(1) When the customer sought insurance, did the insurer ask a clear question about the matter which is now under dispute?

(2) Did the answer to that clear question induce the insurer~ that is, did it influence the insurer's decision to enter into the contract at all, or to do so under

terms and conditions that it otherwise would not have accepted?

Should the answer to either question be "No", the FOS will not support an insurer in avoiding the policy. Since a question is required before a policy can be avoided, this seems effectively to remove the duty of disclosure.

If the answer to both questions is "Yes", the FOS determines the dispute by consideration of the state of mind of the policyholder at the time any misrepresentation or nondisclosure occurred. The FOS has established four categories:

Deliberate

Customers *deliberately* mislead the insurer if they dishonestly provide information they know to be untrue or incomplete. If the dishonesty is intended to deceive the insurer into giving them an advantage to which they are not entitled, then this is also a fraud and – strictly speaking – the insurance premium does not have to be returned.

Reckless

Customers also breach their duty of good faith if they mislead the insurer by *recklessly* giving answers without caring whether those answers are true or false. An example of recklessness might be where a customer signs a blank proposal form and leaves it to be filled out by someone else. The customer has signed a declaration that *'the above answers are true to the best of my knowledge and belief'*, but does not know what those answers will be. Inadvertent

A customer may also have acted in good faith if their nondisclosure is made *inadvertently*. These are the most difficult cases to determine and involve distinguishing between behaviour that is merely careless and that which amounts to recklessness. Both are forms of negligence.

Innocent

Customers act in good faith if their nondisclosure is made *innocently*.

This may happen because the question is unclear or ambiguous, or because the relevant information is not something that they should reasonably know. In these cases, the insurer will not be able to 'avoid' the contract and (subject to the policy terms and conditions) should pay the claim in full.

There are significant differences between this categorisation and the traditional legal analysis. Lawyers would regard both the deliberate and the reckless categories as being fraud, and the inadvertent category as being negligence. Only the innocent category is common to both approaches.

However, the cases we saw in our research project left us with the clear impression that the FOS takes a wider view of recklessness than might be suggested by the definition quoted above. In practice the FOS distinguishes between two forms of negligence serious negligence which it treats as recklessness and minor negligence which it treats as inadvertence. This distinction allows the FOS to reach a fair and reasonable result in cases of mere carelessness, where avoidance would seem an excessive remedy.

Deliberate or Reckless

Where a misrepresentation or nondisclosure is deliberate or reckless, the FOS allows an insurer to avoid the policy and to refuse to pay any claim.

Case Study

Mr W notified his household insurer that cracks had developed in the walls of his home. Investigations indicated that the cracks resulted from subsidence. At the time Mr W took out the policy, he had informed the insurer that the property had never been affected by movement of any kind, including subsidence, heave, landslip or settlement.

In fact, when Mr W purchased the property the surveyor had reported that: The property is affected by structural movement evident in severe cracking to the gable elevation. This appears significant and likely to be progressive.

The insurer avoided the policy on the basis of the misrepresentation by Mr W. It declined to pay the subsidence claim.

The FOS concluded that the question regarding movement was clear, and that Mr W's reply had not fairly represented the true picture. It supported the insurer in its decision to avoid the policy.

Other than where there is clear evidence of fraud, the FOS requires an insurer to refund the premiums if it avoids a policy.

Inadvertent

Potentially the most difficult category is that of inadvertent misrepresentation. The attempt to distinguish between different forms of negligence can introduce considerable complexity into the analysis. During our research project we encountered many different factual situations in the cases referred to the FOS. It was on occasion hard to predict how a case fitted into the FOS categories. For example, consumers may:

(1) fail to read the question (either reasonably if the form is badly set out, or negligently).

(2) fail to understand the question (because the question is unclear, or they had limited knowledge of such matters, or they acted negligently).

(3) understand the question, but have no way of knowing the answer.

(4) understand the question, and think they know the answer, but give an inaccurate reply (either innocently, or without conducting proper checks, or deliberately).

(5) understand the question, but fail to take enough care with the reply because they didn't realise it mattered.

Nevertheless, as we will see below distinguishing between serious negligence and minor negligence allows the FOS to take a more graduated approach than, say, ICOB, which specifically permits insurers to apply the full remedy of avoidance to all negligent misrepresentations.

Innocent

In cases of innocent misrepresentation or nondisclosure, the insurer is not permitted to avoid the policy, and will be required to meet any claim in full.

Case Study

Mrs B claimed under her motor insurance policy when her son, a named driver, was involved in an accident. On the claim form she disclosed that she had "access" to another car. The insurer pointed out that when she had applied for the policy, two years earlier, she had declared that she did not have the "use" of another car. Had it been aware of the true position it would have increased the premium. On the basis of the apparent misrepresentation the insurer cancelled the policy, rejected the claim and denied liability for damage to the third party vehicle.

The FOS was not satisfied that asking Mrs B if she had "use of another car" was a clear question. Mrs B had interpreted it as asking whether she wanted the policy to cover more than one car. The FOS therefore instructed the insurer to deal with the claim and pay Mrs B a further £200 compensation for its mishandling of the matter.

One curious feature of the FOS approach is that it appears to disregard the issue of materiality. The FOS looks to see whether a clear question about the matter was asked not whether the matter was material. However, the FOS has confirmed to us that it would not allow avoidance for a nonmaterial misrepresentation.

In Ombudsman News Issue 27, the FOS stated:

We may consider whether the firm gave any warning about the consequences of giving false or incomplete information, and how clear such a warning was.

Presumably the lack of such warnings might, in some cases, be enough to tip the scales and lead the FOS to conclude that a misrepresentation was, say, inadvertent rather than reckless.

A graduated approach to remedies in cases of "inadvertence"

In cases of what it terms inadvertence, the FOS considers the terms the insurer would have offered had it been aware of the true position. This could lead to a number of outcomes. For example:

(1) If the insurer would have refused the application for insurance, it will be allowed to avoid the policy and refuse to pay any claim.

(2) If the insurer would have applied an exclusion to the cover, the policy will be rewritten to include this term. In some cases this will entitle the insurer to refuse to pay any claim that has arisen.

(3) If the insurer would have simply charged a higher premium, a proportionate settlement of any claim

. may be appropriate. In its simplest form this might mean that a policyholder who has only paid, say, 60% of the correct premium only gets 60% of the claim paid.

Case Study

Mrs A claimed under her motor policy when her car was stolen. The insurer discovered that she had not declared four convictions for speeding. These were relatively minor matters, and if disclosed would have led to a premium loading of 12% initially, reducing to 5% for the second year of cover. The insurer exercised its legal right to avoid her policy and decline the theft claim.

The FOS considered that the question asked by the insurer about convictions was clear. However, it felt that the nondisclosure by Mrs A was an oversight. It concluded that a fair and reasonable settlement would be for the insurer to meet the claim on a proportional basis. The insurer agreed to pay Mrs A 85% of the value of her claim.

RENEWALS

The FOS generally expects an insurer to ask clear questions if it wishes to obtain information from a policyholder at renewal. It points out that asking simply whether anything has changed is unlikely to produce reliable results unless the policyholder is provided with copies of the original information: Customers cannot bc expected to remember all the details of information they provided perhaps several years earlier. So if firms ask them general questions such as 'has anything changed in the information we asked for in your proposal form?' when they are renewing a policy, the responses are unlikely to be reliable... If a firm wants policyholders to check and reconfirm all the information they provided originally, then it is good practice for the firm to send them a copy of that information, or to ask all the questions afresh. A firm that does not follow good practice may not be able to use a customer's failure to provide information as a reason to decline a claim.

CONCLUSION

Where misrepresentation or nondisclosure is alleged, the ABI Statements and FSA Rules may be of assistance to a wellinformed consumer. However, we have no doubt that it is the FOS which ultimately offers the consumer the most valuable protection. In particular, it addresses the harshness of the law in three important ways:

(1) The FOS treats consumers as if there is no residual duty of disclosure. Neither the Statements nor the Rules have this effect.

(2) The FOS will require an insurer to settle claims on a proportionate basis where there has been "inadvertent" misrepresentation and the insurer, had it been aware of the truth, would simply have accepted the application at an increased premium. In contrast, both Statements and Rules allow avoidance for "negligent" misrepresentation.

(3) The FOS does not offer an insurer any remedy in cases of innocent misrepresentation. It appears to take this line regardless whether there has been a claim or not whereas corresponding provisions in the Statements and Rules only apply where a claim has been made.

5

CONSUMER INSURANCE – THE CASE FOR LAW REFORM

INTRODUCTION

Fairness and Reasonable Expectations

The Law Commission's 1980 report and the others that followed it identified a number of ways in which the law is unfair. It is not suggested that insureds are being cheated~ the market for insurance is highly competitive and no doubt they get value for money. What seems unfair about the law is that it defeats the reasonable expectations of consumers. Insurance is intended to be an effective risktransfer mechanism, bringing peace of mind to the purchaser. The consumer exchanges the risk of a loss of unknown amount for the payment of a known premium. This process performs a valuable function in enabling consumers to plan their financial affairs prudently.

Where claims are not met, the transfer of risk fails, and the peace of mind has proved to be illusory. In some cases, the results can be devastating for consumers. For example, in our study of FOS cases we were struck by the large number of complaints we saw relating to critical illness policies. Consumers who were already suffering from their own serious illhealth, or that of a family member, were faced with the added stress of having a claim declined. The problem is not restricted to critical illness policies. We found evidence of many different types of policy being avoided in circumstances where this approach seemed unduly harsh.

It seems correct to allow a policy to be avoided where the policyholder has behaved fraudulently when taking it out. 1 However, as the FOS said in its response to our Scoping Paper: Only a relatively small proportion of policyholders who have failed to disclose relevant information are found to have done so with any dishonest intent. We are chiefly concerned with those who were not fraudulent. It is arguable that they deserve better protection than the law currently provides – and that (were they aware of the problem) consumer insureds generally would want that better protection even at the price of slightly increased premiums.

Confidence in the Market Place

It is not just the individual insured with whom we need to be concerned. Where insurance fails to meet reasonable expectations, confidence in the market can be undermined. Dissatisfied consumers spread the word, and those who have had an insurance claim rejected frequently have a deep sense of grievance.

We are concerned that the bad press from which insurers sometimes suffer must inevitably deter consumers from purchasing insurance when it would be in their best interests to do so. It is clear from the comments we have received that some insurers share this concern.

ARE THE FOS AND THE FSA RULES A SUBSTITUTE FOR LAW REFORM?

In Part 4 we showed that whilst the Statements of Practice, the COB and ICOB Rules may assist consumers in cases of misrepresentation or nondisclosure, it is the FOS scheme that offers the most effective remedy. We now turn to assess whether the FOS and the FSA Rules are an adequate substitute for law reform.

From a complainant's perspective, the FOS offers many advantages over the alternative of court action:

(1) Compulsory jurisdiction complaints are determined by reference to what is "fair and reasonable in all the circumstances of the case".

(2) The service is free to complainants.

(3) The FOS can provide remedies not available through the courts. For example, it may instruct an insurer to reinstate a policy, or to rewrite it on different terms.

(4) An application to the FOS is a "no lose" option for complainants. If a complainant accepts the ombudsman's decision it becomes binding on both insurer and complainant. However, the complainant is free to reject the decision and pursue the matter through the courts.

(5) The FOS processes are intended to be relatively rapid.

(6) The FOS has an inquisitorial process. Once a case is accepted for investigation, the FOS will carry out its own investigations rather than merely relying on the arguments presented by the parties.

(7) The FOS has introduced several initiatives to make its service more accessible to complainants. It maintains an informative website and a range of publications. Last year it demonstrated that it was capable of conducting "correspondence in Arabic, phone calls in Tagalog and emails in Urdu".

(8) The processes operated by the FOS are intended to be informal and friendly. There is no need for a complainant to be represented.

(9) The FOS has more experience than the courts in dealing with the types of insurance dispute within its jurisdiction. Importantly, it may also be more aware of current issues within the insurance industry, and have a better understanding of the problems typically faced by complainants.

(10) The FOS is not bound by the rules that would apply in court proceedings. It may exclude evidence that would be admitted in court, and admit evidence that would be excluded.

(11) The FOS will take into account the provisions of both ABI Statements. Even though SGIP has been withdrawn, the FOS treats it as an indicator of good practice.

Similarly, the COB and ICOB Rules potentially offer consumers greater protection than the strict law.

However, we do not consider that the FOS and the FSA Rules, separately or together, are a satisfactory alternative to law reform for consumers. We have two main groups of concerns. The first group are about substance: do the FOS and FSA Rules in fact protect consumers fully, or is it necessary to change the law? The second group are about the current state of "the law as a whole", i.e. the general rules plus the FOS and FSA Rules.

The FOS cannot in Practice Protect all Consumers

As to the substance, we think there are probably still serious gaps in coverage.

On the one hand, our research and concerns expressed to us by the industry itself suggest that there are some insurers who are still refusing to pay claims and avoiding polices when that is not consistent with the Statements of Practice or would not be permitted by the FOS. Given the obscurity of the statements, FSA Rules and the detail of the

FOS approach, many insurers simply decide cases on the basis of the strict law. Our survey of ombudsman cases showed that many insurers did in fact apply the law in this way. This penalises the many consumer and small businesses who do not take their cases to the FOS. On the other hand, it suggests that not every case is being dealt with or prevented by the FOS. If consumers go to the FOS, their case will be dealt with in a way that is helpful, fair and (subject to the gaps we identify below) meets reasonable expectations. However, the consumer must get to the FOS. It is no criticism of the scheme to say that it does not reach everyone. Among the applicants to the FOS, some groups are underrepresented.

So our first concern is simply that there are still claims being dealt with under the strict law and that by no means all cases will get to the FOS. It is likely that there are consumer insureds whose claims are not being paid when generally accepted good practice and the FOS guidance suggest that they should be.

There might of course be some worthy claims that would not be paid even if the law were brought into line with the FOS guidance. On occasions, insurers' employees may misunderstand the law or simply make wrong decisions. The problem must be much worse, however, when the law says one thing and the rules of practice another. The employee might quite reasonably believe that they are doing the right thing in applying the letter of the law.

FSA Rules are Unlikely to Achieve Protection Either

In principle, the COB and ICOB Rules should prevent insurers from turning down claims when the consumer has acted reasonably. Again, however, we doubt whether all insurers will always follow the COB and ICOB all the time. The gap between them and the law is an invitation to make mistakes.

There is a further problem that the FSA Rules are less demanding than the FOS. For example, as we saw earlier, ICOB merely requires that the consumer be warned about the duty to disclose. The FOS effectively dispenses with it: if the insurer wants a piece of information, it should ask for it. Another example is that COB and ICOB Rules permit the insurer to avoid the policy if the consumer's misrepresentation or nondisclosure was careless, whereas the FOS requires payment of a proportionate part of the claim. Not only do these differences invite further confusion but they mean that the FSA Rules will not protect the consumer fully. Further, although in principle a breach of the COB or ICOB Rules may lead to the insurer being liable for breach of statutory duty, we doubt the practical efficacy of this remedy save when a very large sum is at stake.

Clarity and Accessibility

Turning now to the state of "the law as a whole", we have equally serious concerns. The first is simply that the present position is increasingly incoherent. There is a growing gulf between unsatisfactory law on the one hand and the patchwork of Statements of Practice, FSA Rules and guidance from the FOS on the other. In some cases, the different elements of this patchwork may each give different and conflicting results to a question. Take, for example, a basic issue: is an insurer required to ask an applicant for insurance any questions?

(1) The law provides that an insurer is not obliged to ask an applicant for insurance any questions. It can simply rely on the duty of disclosure by which the applicant is bound.

(2) Both SGIP and SLIP do require the insurer ask questions about matters "generally found to be material". However, no sanction is provided if this requirement is breached.

(3) Neither ICOB nor COB contain specific Rules requiring the asking of questions, though an insurer may need to ask questions to meet its other obligations under the Rules.

(4) The FOS does not explicitly require questions to be asked. However, that is the practical effect since it will not allow an insurer to avoid a policy for nondisclosure as opposed to misrepresentation.

The existence of these conflicting sources of law and practice make it unnecessarily difficult for insurers and policyholders to establish their respective rights. The multiple layers of regulation, and to some extent the lack of precision in the rules of each layer, cause serious and quite unnecessary confusion. We believe that the situation has reached a stage where it can only be resolved by law reform.

Denial of a Remedy in Court

We think that the FOS provides an extremely valuable service. However, we do not think that it should be the only way in which consumers can secure justice. We believe it is unacceptable that if the courts are asked to resolve a consumer case they may be required to apply unfair and archaic legal rules. Whilst we accept that most consumer cases will be resolved through the FOS, there are circumstances in which a consumer may reasonably choose to pursue a dispute through the courts. For example:

(1) The amount of the dispute may exceed £100,000, the limit on binding awards that can be made by the FOS (nonbinding recommendations can be made for any sum in excess of £100,000).

(2) The FOS may have declined to deal with the case on any one of eighteen grounds listed in Rule 3.3 of the DISP Sourcebook of the FSA Handbook. We are told

by the FOS that the Rule has a significant impact: One of the principal reasons that we decline to look at a case is that we regard it as more suitable for a decision in the courts. This is frequently the case where the assessment of the evidence requires crossexamination of third parties.

This creates a whole category of cases to which our process is unsuited. In declining to consider such cases, due perhaps to their reliance on the evidence of a third party (which may include a broker or intermediary or the departed salesman or representative of a firm), we must accept that, in relation to nondisclosure, the effect of a referral to the courts is that the case will be decided upon an entirely different basis.

This basis is one that we do not regard as fair or reasonable or as representing good practice in the sector. In other words if the insurer can justifiably demand that they are able to cross examine a third party then they may win a nondisclosure case that they would otherwise have lost at the FOS.

(3) The consumer may have rejected a decision from the FOS in the hope of obtaining a more favourable result by litigation.

The FOS points out that there is a further problem in that its existence may have stunted the development of the law: We are concerned that the development of the common law has been impeded by our activities and by the very limited chance of success that any consumer may have in pursuing a nondisclosure case or misrepresentation issue in the courts.

Furthermore the FOS is conscious that the current position may bring positive benefits to insurers with lower standards: At present any insurer operating to good industry practice or to an even more enlightened standard for consumers is conscious that they can be undermined in pricing or cost terms by any insurer who chooses to offer a service that is strictly in accordance with the law.

The insurer offering to meet only the minimum of legal obligations is protected by the privacy offered by the FOS process and by the difficulty that consumers and their legal advisers may have in attempting to assert legal rights that are novel in insurance law terms The "effective law" is discretionary

We believe that it is undesirable that the FOS is routinely obliged to replace the most fundamental principles of insurance contract law with its own approach.

There are two obvious objections to this position:

(1) The FOS may develop its approach without public debate or wide consultation.
(2) As the FOS is able to change its approach at will, there is a continuing degree of uncertainty.

The Risk of Legal Challenge

We have also been told of concerns, even among the Ombudsmen themselves, that the gap between the approach being applied by the FOS and the underlying law is becoming so wide that they fear a legal challenge. Whether or not that is realistic, it would be unfortunate if the FOS or individual Ombudsmen feel restricted in how far they can make insurers adhere to good practice and to depart from the strict law because of the threat of legal challenge.

CONCLUSION: AN INCOHERENT AND FLAWED SYSTEM

The present system is unsatisfactory in four ways:

(1) *It fails to prevent some insurers avoiding policies inappropriately*. Insurers may repudiate claims for

negligent misstatements that have nothing to do with the claim in issue.

(2) *It is inaccessible and obscure.* To understand how the current law works, insurers and consumer advisers need to work through multiple layers of law, selfregulation, regulation and ombudsman case law. Not only do the rules differ but the meaning of some of the individual rules, and thus the differences intended, are unclear. It is hardly surprising that insurers often do not understand the rules that govern this area, and attempt to avoid policies inappropriately.

(3) *Consumers are deprived of a genuine choice between the FOS and the courts.* Except in limited circumstances (see paragraph 5.19 above), no welladvised consumer would choose to take a case to court, because a court would be forced to apply the full rigour of the law.

(4) *It requires the FOS to exercise undue discretion.* Instead of using its discretion to supplement the law, the FOS has been required to develop its approach almost from first principles. The FSA Rules provide little assistance – the FOS has confirmed to us that COB and ICOB "do not and are not intended to deal with anything like the breadth and extent of disputes that arise in insurance policies".

We conclude that the time has come to state clearly what rights and obligations a consumer insured should have. We believe strongly that a new statute should replace the current patchwork by a single system that is coherent and clear, and that is fair in that it meets the reasonable expectations of both consumers and insurers.

6

CONSUMERS – OUR PROPOSALS IN DETAIL

INTRODUCTION

We think there is a strong case for reform of consumer insurance contract law. In our view, a new statute should:

(1) redefine what is and what is not a material fact in terms of what the reasonable consumer will think is material~

(2) provide that avoidance is appropriate only to fraud, and clarify what amounts to fraud for these purposes~

(3) exclude a remedy to the insurer where the consumer has acted innocently but not negligently~

(4) clarify the remedies that should be applied in cases of negligent misrepresentation~

(5) abolish the requirement that consumers should volunteer information.

In addition, "basis of the contract" clauses should be rendered ineffective. This would prevent insurers from evading the scheme by converting the answers in proposal forms into contractual warranties.

The new law should be mandatory – it should not be possible for the parties to contract out of it to the detriment of the consumer. We have reached this conclusion for the same reasons that lead us to believe that consumers should be treated differently from businesses. In particular, consumers are unlikely to have the knowledge or bargaining power to allow for meaningful negotiations with insurers. There is therefore a real risk that contractingout would be imposed upon them. We tentatively propose that it should not be possible to contract out of the new rules governing consumer insurance except in favour of the consumer.

Below we set out tentative proposals on these issues. The fact that most consumer proposal forms now ask detailed questions means that misrepresentation is now of greater relevance than nondisclosure, which has become almost a residual issue. We therefore consider first materiality in the context of misrepresentation, and the remedies for misrepresentation, before we discuss whether there should be a duty of disclosure on consumer insureds.

We note at the outset that there is some overlap between these various issues. If, for example, there is to be no remedy for an innocent misrepresentation by the consumer, it may be that there is no need for a separate rule on materiality. A consumer who reasonably thought that any incompleteness or inaccuracy in his answer was not material might simply be treated as making only an innocent misrepresentation. However, there may be cases in which the two do not overlap and for purposes of the discussion we treat them separately.

We have found the general law of misrepresentation, and in particular the Misrepresentation Act 1967, of little assistance in developing our proposals. The right to damages for negligent misrepresentation conferred by section 2(1), and the power of the court under section 2(2) to refuse to permit rescission and to award damages in lieu, were designed for contracts such as sale. They cannot readily be applied to the very different risks and rewards of insurance contracts. In insurance contracts, risks are spread across a pool of contracts, so it may be inappropriate to look only at the atypical contract where a claim has arisen. For example, where an insurer would have charged a higher premium it may not be appropriate to compensate the insurer by awarding it damages equivalent to the difference between the premium paid and the premium it would have charged had it known the truth. This does not compensate the insurer for the lower premium it has received in cases where no claim has been made. It makes more sense to reduce the insured's claim proportionally. We therefore think that insurance contracts continue to require principles of misrepresentation specific to them.

At the end of this Part we consider a number of additional issues related to misrepresentation and nondisclosure which were not covered by the 1980 Report or the FSA and the FOS schemes.

THE TEST OF MATERIALITY

In our view, the test of materiality requires reform as it applies to consumer insurance. The matter should be looked at primarily from the point of view of the person on whom the duty falls: that is, a reasonable insured. The reformulation should apply to cases of misrepresentation and — if it were to be decided that a duty of disclosure should be retained in consumer cases — to nondisclosure.

It should be noted that in some jurisdictions, e.g. France and Norway, in the field of general consumer insurance, less emphasis is put on materiality. In both these jurisdictions, misrepresentation is the prominent, or in the case of France, the only cause of action. The test is simply that the questions posed be answered truthfully (in France) and completely and exhaustively (Norway). However, we think that a materiality test is important for both misrepresentation and nondisclosure, in order to try to give some certainty as to what is or is not required on the insured.

Alternative Formulations

We believe that the test of materiality should be considered from the point of view of the reasonable consumer. The question is how to formulate the rule. Several proposals have been made along these lines. Below we consider various formulations and the issues they raise.

In 1957, the Law Reform Committee formulated a new definition of materiality, stating that for the purposes of any contract of insurance no fact should be deemed material unless it would have been considered material by a reasonable insured.

In 1980, the English Law Commission supported a similar policy outcome, though the structure of their formulation was different. It recommended that the definition of a material fact "should remain substantially the same as in the present law". However, an insured's duty of disclosure should be limited to a fact which:

(1) is material to the risk

(2) is either known to the applicant or is one which he can be assumed to know, and

(3) is one which a reasonable man in the position of the applicant would disclose to his insurers, having regard to the nature and extent of the insurance cover which is sought and the circumstances in which it is sought.

More recently, in *Cuthbertson v Friends' Provident Life Office,* Lord Eassie set out the test that applies to life insurance in Scotland:

(1) For any fact to be material, it must be material in the view of the reasonable underwriter " If the fact

were regarded by such an underwriter as of no significance, *cadit quaestio.*"

(2) Additionally, the insurer must show that either:

(a) "The proposer appreciated that the fact in question would have had that significance", or, assuming the proposer did not have that appreciation,

(b) "A reasonable person making the proposal and possessed with the factual knowledge possessed by the actual proposer would think that fact to be material to the insurer".

Discussion of these Formulations

All these proposals share a common policy purpose, namely to limit the insured's duty of disclosure to facts which a reasonable insured would think relevant. However, when one looks at the three formulations in depth, several issues emerge.

Subjective and Objective Formulations

In Australia, as the Insurance Contracts Act 1984 was passing through the Commonwealth Parliament, there was considerable debate over how far a reasonable insured test should take into account the circumstances of the particular policyholder in question. A draft which originally looked at what "a person in the circumstances of the insured could reasonably be expected to know" was changed to reflect what "a reasonable person in the circumstances could be expected to know".

Although the words seem similar, they represent different tests. The first looks at the particular idiosyncrasies of the insured, taking into account (for example) their age, education, and knowledge of English. The second sets up a more objective standard. For example, a "reasonable insured" may know that if an insurer has asked about signs of subsidence it will wish to know about a lengthening crack over the front door. However, a policyholder who has just been bereaved and always left home maintenance to their spouse may quite reasonably not realise the significance of such damage.

There is a difficult policy balance here. The insurer cannot be expected to know about every idiosyncrasy of every insured. It cannot know that the person completing the form has suffered bereavement, or understands very little about house maintenance or medical terms. On the other hand, it seems harsh to penalise a policyholder for falling below some objective standard, when this was quite reasonable given their particular circumstances.

In deciding what a reasonable insured would know, we think the courts should take into account all the circumstances known to the insurer, including the type of policy, the way the policy was advertised and sold, and the normal characteristics of those sort of policyholders. We think it important that the standard is not set too high. It should be assessed from the point of view of ordinary, normal, fallible people – not some idealised perfection.

To take an extreme example, we have been told that there has been at least one scheme to sell insurance by text message. The constraints of this medium may significantly affect what may be expected from applicants.

What we find more difficult is whether the test should take into account facts which the insurer would not necessarily have known about, such as the insured's stressful family circumstances or lack of education. This was the effect of the first Australian draft.

We think that it may be possible to achieve a workable compromise. The insurer cannot be expected to make allowances for particular characteristics of which it does not know. If however the insurer actually knows of the particular problems faced by the insured – for example, the proposal is made over the phone and it is evident that the proposer speaks very little English, or if the insured explains that she knows nothing about medical terms and asks for help – the reasonableness of the insured's understanding of what they were being asked for should be judged accordingly. That fits with the notion of "know your customer". In discussions the FOS supported this approach: In so far as factors of age, infirmity, limited mental capacity, poor command of language or limited literacy are known to the insurer then there would seem to be a strong public policy argument for the law not permitting the insurer to simply ignore these characteristics of their customers.

The Nature of the Evidence

At present, the issue of what is material to a "prudent underwriter" is often determined by expert evidence from the industry. In 1980, the Law Commission saw the prominence granted to insurers' evidence as a serious criticism of the current law.

Under our proposed reform, the actual insurer in question will need to start by showing that the issue was material to them, in that if they had known the truth they would not have entered into the same contract on the same terms.

An alternative approach would be to follow up the idea that materiality should be judged by what the insurer knows about the particular consumer. Such knowledge may allow the insurer to judge the extent to which the consumer will understand what information is required. A revised test of materiality might therefore ask whether a reasonable insurer with the same knowledge of the client as the actual insurer would expect the consumer to understand that a particular matter was relevant. That would once more be a question on which the court might hear evidence from underwriters and brokers.

The Position of a Niche Insurer

A further criticism of the present test of materiality is that in some circumstances it may prove unfair to an innovative insurer. As discussed above, some insurers may wish to develop niche markets, by asking questions that seem irrelevant to the generality of insurers. For example, an insurer may assess risk on the basis that all their policyholders are members of a particular profession or union. This means that a question about occupation may be material to them, even if it is irrelevant to most prudent underwriters. The insurer may ask a clear question, which succeeds in communicating the importance of the question to a reasonable policyholder. However, if the policyholder gives a negligent answer, the insurer may be without a remedy. As we pointed out earlier, it is possible that it will fail the first limb of the *Pan Atlantic* test because the representation would not influence the judgement of the hypothetical prudent insurer, as required by section 20(2) of the Marine Insurance Act 1906. This point, implicit within the 1980 test, is made explicit in *Cuthbertson.*

The law of New York favours the niche insurer with its test of materiality. The test is concerned solely with the effect the nondisclosure or misrepresentation has on that particular insurer. This test clearly favours the insurer as it is coupled with the fact that even a slight change in the resulting contract can lead to the harshest of remedies. However, it is recognised that the principle of measuring materiality with reference to the specific insurer in question has its merits.

We wonder whether in such circumstances insurers require greater protection than they currently receive under section 20(2) of 1906 Act. One possible approach which might provide such protection would be to define a fact as material if it is material to the particular insurer, and a reasonable insured would understand it to be material to that insurer, even if other underwriters would not regard it as such.

This would suggest a twopart test. Initially, the actual insurer would need to prove that the issue was material to them, in that had it known the true facts it would not have entered into the same contract on the same terms. This is no different to the current law's requirement that the insurer prove inducement. Once this had been established, the focus would then shift to the insured.

As with *Cuthbertson*, if "the proposer appreciated that the fact in question would have had that significance", that would be the end of the matter. Otherwise the court has to ask what a reasonable insured would have understood to be material in the circumstances, given the nature of the policy, the way that it was sold and the questions that were asked (or whatever variant of the "reasonable insured" test is adopted).

CONCLUSION

Our tentative proposal is that insurers should only be entitled to a remedy for an insured's nondisclosure or misrepresentation in so far as this is material, as defined below. The same test should apply to misrepresentation and nondisclosure.

(1) First, the actual insurer must show inducement, in that had it known the true facts it would not have entered into the same contract on the same terms or at all.

(2) Additionally, the insurer must show either

(a) that the proposer appreciated that the fact in question would have that significance or, if not,

(b) that a reasonable insured in the circumstances would have appreciated its significance.

In assessing what a reasonable insured would appreciate, the courts should take into account the type of policy, the way the policy was advertised and sold, and the normal characteristics of consumers in the market.

We ask whether the test should also take into account any particular characteristics or circumstances affecting the insured, so far as these were known to the insurer. However, they would not look at individual circumstances, known only to the insured.

We see this new test (in whichever formulation) as having two advantages. First, it will provide a fairer balance of rights between insurers and insured, by asking what the proposer did or should have appreciated in the circumstances. Secondly, it will provide greater protection to innovative insurers, who rely on matters that most underwriters in the market do not rely on.

REMEDIES

In our view the remedy available should differ according to the state of mind or conduct of the insured. This is in line with other jurisdictions. Below we distinguish between behaviour that is fraudulent, innocent but negligent and innocent without negligence. Avoidance is appropriate where the insured has behaved fraudulently. Where the insured has behaved both innocently and reasonably, we think that insurers should take policyholders as they find them. In the midrange cases, where the insured has behaved carelessly or negligently, the law should as far as possible put the parties into the position in which they would have been had the facts been stated correctly. Depending on the circumstances, this could mean that the claim may be rejected or that it should be paid in part.

Fraudulent Conduct

Where an insured has behaved fraudulently, it is right that a high penalty should be imposed, even to the extent of overcompensating the insurer for the loss they have suffered. As Lord Steyn put it, a generous measure of damages indicates that the defendant is morally reprehensible and it aims to deter wrongdoing. However, if the law is to impose a penalty of this type, the category must be defined carefully so that it includes only those who are morally blameworthy.

The standard definition of fraud, as set out in *Derry v Peek*, is that the representor must either know that the statement is false or have "no care whether it is true or false". Lord Bramwell was careful to distinguish a lack of interest in whether the statement is true (which is reckless) from "a lack of reasonable ground for believing it to be true" (which is merely negligent).

For present purposes we also think that the insured must know both that the information it gives is inaccurate (or realise that it may be inaccurate and not care) and that the issue is material (or realise that it may be material and not care). We have come across many cases where a policyholder knew that an answer was not strictly accurate, but thought that the answer was irrelevant.

For example, we were told about a motorist who filled in a proposal form that asked whether his family owned another car. He thought it was a marketing question. He was happy with the insurance arrangements on the other car, and did not want to be sent junk mail about it. He therefore answered no. If he had been wrong about the significance of the question, he may have acted carelessly or even foolishly, but we do not think this behaviour carries the moral blameworthiness necessary to be classified as fraud.

Our survey of ombudsman cases also revealed cases where policyholders failed to tell insurers about what they perceived as minor medical matters because they did not think they mattered. We came across several cases where people had said they had not suffered from stress, anxiety or depression when their medical notes revealed otherwise. For example, one woman had taken time off work for stress, but saw this as related to her matrimonial problems rather than her health. She said that she did not think that it was a medical issue relevant to her application for life insurance. If this were true, she may have been seriously mistaken and negligent, but she was not acting fraudulently.

We tentatively propose that insurers should be allowed to avoid policies where the insured has acted fraudulently at the precontractual stage, that is, if the insured:

(1) knew that the statement was untrue (or realised that it might be not be true and did not care) and

(2) knew that the statement was material to the insurer (or realised that it might be material and did not care whether it was or not).

We note that the Australian Law Reform Commission also recommended that insurers should retain the right to avoid a policy for fraud. However, they thought that in some circumstances avoidance could be seriously disproportionate to the harm suffered by the insurer. They therefore recommended that courts should have a discretion not to avoid, but instead adjust the rights of the parties, having regard to all relevant facts, including the need to deter fraudulent behaviour. 10 In our view, this recommendation is excessively lenient on fraudulent behaviour, and we do not recommend introducing such a provision in Britain.

Other than the Australian provision mentioned above, the jurisdictions examined have unanimously treated fraudulent behaviour harshly.

Innocent Conduct

We have already indicated that a claim should not be defeated because of an inaccurate answer or a failure to disclose information if the consumer honestly and reasonably thought that the information stated inaccurately or not disclosed was not material. The same approach should apply when the consumer knows or should know that the information is material but is innocent in other ways. Thus when the insured makes an incorrect statement of fact which is clearly material but does so without any negligence – for example, because they were merely passing on information given them by their surveyor and therefore they had reasonable grounds for believing what they said to be true – we think that insurer should not be entitled to avoid the policy or refuse to pay the claim.

It should be noted that in France and Australia the need to consider innocence is dispensed with. These jurisdictions define the offences such that without actual knowledge of the information allegedly not disclosed or misrepresented, there is no claim.

COMPARISONS TO STATEMENTS OF OPINION

The law already goes some way to protect those who act innocently. As we have seen, for the purposes of misrepresentation, the Marine Insurance Act 1906 makes a distinction between facts and opinions. Where the misrepresentation is deemed to be one of fact, an insurer may avoid for any material inaccuracy, even if the policyholder had no way of knowing that what they said was untrue. However, where it is deemed a matter of opinion, then the insurer is without a remedy unless it can prove that the policyholder acted in bad faith. The policy may not be avoided because the insured had no reasonable grounds for their belief. So a statement of opinion which is honestly held is not treated as a misrepresentation, and a statement of fact that is clearly about something not within the insured's knowledge is often treated as one of opinion.

The ABI Statement of General Insurance Practice ("SGIP") also considered that it should be sufficient for a consumer to fill in the form according to their own knowledge and belief. The first paragraph states: The declaration at the foot of the proposal form should be restricted to completion according to the proposer's knowledge and belief. The clear implication is that statements about matters which the insured cannot know should not give rise tc a remedy. The insured is treated as acting innocently and the insurer should not be entitled to avoid the policy and reject the claim.

The law on nondisclosure is different. The starting principle is that one need only disclose what one knows. However, under section 18(1) of the Marine Insurance Act 1906, the insured is "deemed to know every circumstance which, in the ordinary course of business, ought to be known by him". This means that where an insured fails to mention something they ought to know, an insurer may succeed in an action for nondisclosure, even though it would fail under misrepresentation on the grounds the opinion was genuine. But this would only happen in business cases. In *Economides*, the phrase "in the ordinary course of business" was interpreted literally as applying only to business insured rather than consumers. Thus an undervaluation of the property insured, some of which belonged to the proposer's parents, was treated as a mere statement of opinion. So again the law acts to protect the "innocent" consumer insured. Innocent misrepresentations of fact

In contrast, if the insured makes what is clearly a misrepresentation of fact but does so without negligence, the current position is that as a matter of strict law the policy may be avoided. The SGIP, ICOB and the FOS guidance all temper the law in this area.

In our view, the insurer should have no remedy for misrepresentation or a nondisclosure if the insured had reasonable grounds for believing the truth of what they said. We think this is uncontroversial. It reflects accepted industry practice, FSA regulation, and current FOS decisions. It also aligns more closely the current tests for misrepresented facts and incorrect opinions.

Other Forms of Innocent Behaviour

Earlier we pointed out that a consumer insured may make other kinds of "innocent" mistake. For example, if the proposal form is set out poorly, they might simply miss a question altogether. That might result in them failing to disclose a fact or, depending on the wording of the question, in them "making a statement", that is clearly material and about which they know the truth. 15 Nonetheless, if they took reasonable care and were misled by the form, they are innocent and should be treated as such. This is, we believe, already the position under the Statements of Practice, the FOS scheme, and under the COB and ICOB Rules. The law should be the same.

We tentatively propose that if the consumer insured had reasonable grounds for believing the truth of what they said, or was not negligent in other ways (such as in failing to answer a question), the insurer should have no remedy for misrepresentation or nondisclosure.

Negligent Conduct

Within behaviour that is innocent rather than fraudulent, there lies a broad swathe of negligent conduct–where the policyholder failed to take sufficient care to understand what the insurer wanted to know or to check their facts. Here we think the law should aim to provide a proportionate remedy which, as far as possible, aims to compensate the insurer for the loss it has suffered.

We have noted that the FOS regularly applies proportionate remedies for mere inadvertence – where the consumer did not act deliberately, but failed to mention something they should have known.

We are not proposing to follow the FOS in distinguishing between different types of negligent behaviour, by (for example) classifying "recklessness" separately from "mere inadvertence". We consider this overly complex. Words such as "reckless" can be used in several different ways, and have proved difficult to apply in this context. But we do think that where there was negligence, the insurer should not have an automatic right to avoid. This is in line with other jurisdictions.

We do not see a need to define negligent conduct. Misrepresentations will be treated as negligent if they are not fraudulent but were made without exercise of reasonable care.

A Proportionate Remedy

Where a nondisclosure or misrepresentation has been negligent (rather than fraudulent) the law should aim to place the insured in the position they would have been had they known the true facts, but no better. This means that:

(1) The court should ask what terms the insurer would have offered had the misrepresentation or nondisclosure not occurred. If a claim has already arisen, it may be that it would be excluded under the terms that would have been agreed, or in an extreme case it may be that a policy would not have been offered at all. In such a case the insurer should not have to meet the claim.

(2) If the insurer would have demanded an increase in premium and a claim has arisen, proportionality should be applied. In other words, if the misrepresentation or nondisclosure led to the consumer only paying 50% of the correct premium, the insurer should only have to pay 50% of the claim.

Proportionality has long been used in French law where the insured's bad faith has not been proved. Under Article L1139 of the *Code des Assurances*, where a misrepresentation is discovered after a loss has occurred: the compensation shall be reduced in proportion to the rate of the premiums paid in relation to the rate of premiums that would be owed if the risks had been truthfully and exhaustively declared.

In 1980, the Law Commission rejected proportionality as an option on two main grounds. The first is that an insurer may react to information in a variety of ways: by declining the risk altogether~ by imposing additional warranties~ by imposing an exclusion clause~ or by increasing the "excess" which the insured must bear. The Commission thought that the proportionality principle was only really useful where the insurer would have charged a higher premium.

Secondly, the Commission thought that it would be too difficult to calculate how much the premium would have been in hypothetical circumstances. It argued that tables of tariffs would only be able to assist in straightforward (but unusual) circumstances, where, for example, a life assurance proposer had misstated their age. However, in the usual case where the undisclosed fact is qualitative rather than quantitative in nature – for example, failure to disclose a gastric complaint in an application for life assurance, or nondisclosure of a previous motoring conviction in an application for motor insurance – tables of tariffs will almost certainly be unable to assist, and disputes would proliferate into litigation with the inevitability of conflicting expert evidence about what the notional premium should be. 16 The Commission argued that in France judges often determined a fair deduction as a matter of fact and discretion, rather than arithmetical precision.

We think the 1980 report exaggerated these difficulties. As the National Consumer Council pointed out, the Insurance Ombudsman Bureau applied proportionality, and its current successor, the FOS also does so. We found cases in FOS files where they had no trouble in dealing with an exclusion that would have been added, or in working out the effect on a premium of an additional motoring conviction. The approach appears to have gained acceptance from the industry 17, and we note that it also has the support of the British Insurance Law Association.

However, it is necessary to think through the effect of various scenarios on the remedy available.

EXCLUSIONS

In our survey of FOS files, it was relatively common for insurers to state that had they known about the insured's health problems, they would have excluded a particular condition from cover. The question then becomes what effect would the exclusion have on the claim that has arisen? In several cases, the exclusion did not affect the claim. For example, a claimant who failed to mention her hearing loss later died of leukaemia. The insurer stated that had they known of the hearing problem they would have excluded hearingrelated problems from the cover. Rightly, the insurer was ordered to meet the claim for leukaemia in full. Similarly, a woman who failed to mention back pain following pregnancy later developed (unrelated) breast cancer. The insurer was required to reinstate the policy subject to a back exclusion, and to pay the claim for cancer.

In other cases, a claim may fall within the terms of the exclusion. For example, a complainant who failed to mention an upcoming opthalmological referral later developed a serious eye problem. The FOS instructed the insurer to reinstate the policy, but subject to an exclusion for eye conditions. This meant that the claim was not covered.

In some cases this result may appear harsh on a policyholder who has made a momentary lapse of judgement, and who is deprived of a large claim. However, it is a fair result from the insurer's point of view. And, from the insured's point of view, it is fairer than the current law, which avoids all claims under the policy, whether affected by the nondisclosure or not.

WARRANTIES AND EXCESSES

We did not find any cases where insurers argued that they would have imposed an additional warranty or excess. However, in principle, we see no reason why they could not be dealt with in the same way. The court or ombudsman should ask what the effect would be if the policy were rewritten to include the new terms. If a claim satisfies the new terms, it must be paid.

An Additional Premium

Proportionality works best when there is clear evidence of what the premium would have been. We accept that in some commercial cases the evidence may be disputed, and that precision may not be possible. Instead, the judge will have to work out what seems a reasonable premium given the evidence available.

French commentators admit that there are many cases where the court is unable to put an accurate percentage on the reduction, and the decision has "an element of arbitrariness". 18 However, it is still the best way of redressing the balance between the parties, which has been upset by the false statement,

In our view, it is preferable to allow judges to aim imprecisely at the correct figure, than to apply precisely the wrong one (as where a policy is avoided altogether for a small increase in the premium). There are many occasions in which the courts are forced to place arbitrary figures on the level of damages, particularly in personal injury cases. The level of imprecision involved here would appear to fall within acceptable limits.

Declining the Risk

If the insurer would have declined the risk altogether, the starting point must be that they should not have to meet the claim. In principle, we think it is right to hold insurers to a contract that they would have entered into had they known the true facts, but wrong to force them to abide by a contract they would not have assented to.

This is fair where all reasonable insurers would have declined the risk because they were concerned about the loss that has in fact occurred. However, difficult cases may arise. One is where this insurer would have declined the risk but other insurers would have accepted it (subject to an increase of premium). It is difficult to know what should happen where the particular insurer would have declined the risk completely, but several other insurers would have accepted it for only a moderate increase in premium.

There is also potential for injustice where the loss is unconnected to the risk: where, for example, a proposer failed to mention high blood pressure and was killed in an accident at work.

In France, the judge at first instance may decide on a fair reduction in these circumstances as a matter of fact and discretion.

We would welcome views about whether the courts or the FOS should also have a discretion to mitigate the harsh effects of avoidance in some cases. Such a discretion could be used where the policyholder's negligence was minor, and where the insurer has not suffered substantive prejudice (or where any prejudice that it has suffered could be adequately compensated by a reduction in the claim).

Effect on Future Cover

The foregoing discussion concentrates on claims that have already arisen. We need to consider whether the insurer should also be obliged to remain on cover. Current law allows the claim to be refused because the insurer can avoid the policy as a whole. For inadvertent misrepresentation, current ombudsman practice is to require that the cover continues on amended terms.

We think, on balance, that where the risk would have been declined altogether had the negligent misrepresentation not occurred, the insurer should remain entitled to avoid the policy.

In other cases, the insurer should offer to remain on cover on the terms it would have granted had the negligent misrepresentation not occurred. If a higher premium would have been charged, a pro rata additional premium may be charged to cover the remaining term of the contract. The policyholder should be given the choice of accepting these new terms or cancelling the policy.

Most consumer policies include a cancellation clause – enabling an insurer simply to cancel the policy after paying the claim. It is likely that consumers will be asked in future applications for insurance whether they have had policies cancelled in the past. The cancellation may blight their ability to gain cover. Alternatively, an insurer may choose not to continue on cover at the next renewal date, with similar consequences. We would be concerned if insurers exercised their cancellation rights or their rights at renewal to avoid our proposals and we invite views on these points.

The Position of Third Parties

It has been suggested to us that a proportionate remedy may be inappropriate where a claim has been made in respect of a liability the policyholder has incurred to a third party. The argument is that it seems unfortunate if a third party's ability to recover from a policyholder is adversely affected by the policyholder's misrepresentations to the insurer. We discuss the position of third parties in the context of business insurance in paragraphs 7.88 to 7.92. Our tentative conclusion is the same for consumer insurance that we should not extend the existing rights of third parties. However we welcome views on this issue.

Tentative Proposals

Our tentative proposal is that, in consumer cases, where the proposer has made a negligent misrepresentation, the court should apply a proportionate remedy by asking what the insurer would have done had it known the true facts. In particular:

(1) Where an insurer would have excluded a particular type of claim, the insurer should not be obliged to pay claims that would fall within the exclusion~

(2) Where an insurer would have declined the risk altogether, the claim may be refused~

(3) Where an insurer would have charged more, the claim should be reduced proportionately to the underpayment of premium.

We believe that these proposals will still leave the consumer with a strong incentive to give accurate information.

There are three further issues on which we would welcome advice:

(1) Is there a case for granting the courts or ombudsman some discretion to prevent avoidance where the insurer would have declined the risk but the policyholder's fault is minor, and other insurers would have accepted the risk at a higher premium? This may also apply where the misrepresented fact is unrelated to the claim.

(2) Should insurers be entitled to avoid policies for the future in all cases, or only where they would have declined the risk?

(3) Is it desirable to give greater protection to third parties in the event of misrepresentation by a policyholder?

THE RESIDUAL DUTY OF DISCLOSURE

It is now generally accepted good practice that in consumer insurance, an insurer should ask questions about any material facts it wishes to know. This was set out clearly in the Statements of Insurance Practice.

For longterm insurance Those matters which insurers have commonly found to be material should be the subject of clear questions in proposal forms. For general consumer insurance, the provision is similar: Those matters which insurers have found generally to be material will be the subject of clear questions in proposals forms.

We saw earlier that the FOS enforces these provisions by refusing to avoid a policy for a nondisclosure where no question was asked. In considering a consumer nondisclosure case, the ombudsman will start by asking whether the insurer has provided evidence that it asked a clear question, to which it received an inaccurate response.

Here we consider whether to bring the law into line with industry practice and ombudsman guidance by requiring insurers to ask consumers clear questions about any matter that is material to them. If no question is asked, the insurer would be regarded as having waived its right to such information. Another way of looking at the same issue would be to abolish consumers' residual duty of disclosure. Consumers would only be required to answer accurately the questions they were asked. This is the approach taken in France following amendments made in 1990.

In 1980, the Law Commission argued against abolishing consumers' duty in this way. It gave three main reasons:

(1) Abolition would enable "sharp practice" by consumers. For example, a consumer should not apply for house insurance without disclosing that they had receivea a threat to burn their house down.

(2) Without a duty of disclosure, it would be difficult to grant temporary cover before a proposal form was completed.

(3) The division between consumers and businesses is artificial the dividing line should really be between "professionals" and "nonprofessionals". Special rules for consumers would lead to complex law, as there would then be three categories:

(a) Consumers.

(b) Businesses.

(c) Marine, Aviation and Transport risks ("MAT").

The insurance market has changed considerably since 1980. It is now common for insurance to be sold over the telephone or by the internet in a way that requires policyholders to answer set questions, in some cases with little opportunity or incentive to disclose additional facts. This point was put to us by the FOS: In many sales processes that are conducted over the phone or the internet it is very difficult for a policyholder to disclose additional facts even if they are minded so to do. It would seem inequitable to require the consumer to override the sales process set in place by the insurer in order to fulfil their legal obligations even if they are reminded of them during the course of a phone call or Internet

The FOS takes the approach that consumers do not need to volunteer information. Interestingly, we found a case very similar to the one noted in the 1980 report. The complainant's daughter had split up from her partner, who made various threats against the family. The complainant then decided to take out contents insurance (after five years without it). She was not asked if she had received threats, and she did not mention them. The household was later burgled. The insurer suspected that the expartner had been involved and they attempted to avoid the policy on the grounds that they should have been told about the threats. The Ombudsman decided that as no question has been asked, the insurer could not require the matter to be disclosed. They should pay the claim.

Our tentative view is that in consumer cases the duty to disclose is no longer needed. It would lead to greater complexity to leave differences between the approach taken by the FOS and the rules required by law in the same case. We think the law should now be brought into line with the FOS guidelines. 6.88 Given existing practice, we believe this proposal will be uncontroversial. It has the following advantages:

(1) It would focus the attention of insurers on what they needed to know at the application stage~

(2) It nevertheless leaves insurers free to ask whatever questions they wish, or indeed to choose to ask no questions at all.

(3) It gives applicants for insurance a clear indication of the information that is required from them.

(4) It simplifies the law by bringing substantive law into line with best practice and the FOS guidelines.

Our tentative proposal is that in the consumer market, insurers should ask consumers clear questions about any matter that is material to them and that, if they do not ask questions on a particular point, the insurer should be regarded as having waived its right to such information.

Preventing General Questions

There is a difficult issue about general questions, along the lines of "is there anything else we would want to know?"

As we have seen, proposal forms already include some extremely wide questions. Some of these seem to represent simply bad practice. The following is an example taken from the FOS study, which not only asks the proposer whether they have ever been ill, but also whether they have "a tendency" to be ill. Have you any physical defect or infirmity or is there any ailment or disease from which you suffer or have suffered or to which you have a tendency?

The French have a provision which effectively codifies the position reached through case law. Article L 1123 para 2 provides that if an insurer asks a question expressed in "general terms", it cannot complain when it receives a vague response. Its effect is to discourage insurers from asking vague, openended questions as it could leave them without recourse when a misrepresentation is made.

We see that general questions can have a useful function, particularly if there is no general duty on a consumer insured to disclose material facts that it might never occur to the insurer to ask about – such as the threat to burn down the house. The general question avoids at least the first criticism of the duty to disclose made by the 1980 report, that the consumer may not realise they have such a duty. To that extent, a general question can perform the same function as a warning to the consumer that they have such a duty, as envisaged by the SGIP. The problem with them, however, is that the consumer may be left in doubt as to what is wanted. If they think of something and are in doubt about its materiality, they can ask~ but they may never even think of it despite the general question.

There are two ways of dealing with such questions. The first would be for the court to strike them out, on the ground that unless a question meets a minimum level of precision it should be disregarded. The second would be to permit them but for the court to ask whether a reasonable consumer would understand that this question was asking about this particular information.

For example, taking the question above, it is extremely unclear whether a consumer is expected to mention the ingrowing toenail removed 5 years ago. However, most consumers would realise that they should mention their recent cancer diagnosis. The first approach would strike out the question altogether, with the result that consumers would no longer be required to mention any health issues (including the cancer). The second would absolve a consumer of the requirement to mention the toenail (on the grounds that the insurer did not make this sufficiently clear) but would still require the cancer to be mentioned.

Striking out unclear questions would concentrate insurers' minds on the need to ask for information in a clear, sensible way, but it could lead to surprising decisions in some circumstances. The second approach would do justice in the individual case but does not give insurers such an incentive to clarify their questions. It would also avoid the great difficulty of defining what amounts to a general question for this purpose. Our tentative view is that general questions should be permitted, but that the court should ask whether a reasonable consumer would understand that this question was asking about this particular information.

RENEWALS

Our tentative proposals on misrepresentation and nondisclosure will apply to renewals of policies as much as to new applications. If an insurer requires information from the policyholder at renewal it will therefore need to ask a clear question. Under our proposals there will be no residual duty of disclosure.

In Part 2 we identified one potential pitfall peculiar to renewals – the question which simply asks the policyholder whether there has been any change in circumstances. 22 If the policyholder has not retained or been given a copy of any information previously supplied to the insurer, it may be hard to answer such a question accurately.

We agree with the FOS that good practice dictates that such questions should be accompanied by copies of all the information previously provided to the insurer. However, we would go further and ask whether, for consumer insurances, insurers should lose their rights to rely on nonfraudulent misrepresentations made in response to such questions unless such copies have been provided. In practice we anticipate that the copies could be provided in one of two ways – either as paper or electronic duplicates of the original documents, or as paper or electronic output of data stored on an insurer's computer systems, having been extracted from the original documents.

Our tentative view is that in consumer insurance an insurer should have no right to rely on nonfraudulent misrepresentations made at renewal in response to such a question, unless the policyholder was supplied with copies of any information previously provided to the insurer.

MIDTERM ADJUSTMENTS

The duty of disclosure arises again if there is a mid-term adjustment to a policy — for example, where the policyholder requests an increase to the sum insured. Some policies may also seek to impose a continuing duty of disclosure by contractual term. We intend to deal with these matters in a later paper on postcontractual good faith.

BASIS OF THE CONTRACT CLAUSES

If the law of nondisclosure is reformed, it will also be necessary to consider "basis of the contract" clauses. Without controls on how basis of the contract clauses are used, insurers would be able to evade the reforms we are proposing. We note that SGIP barred the use of basis of the contract clauses in consumer policies, and our present view is that this is a sensible approach. However, we intend to discuss the matter in more detail in our next issues paper.

Our tentative view is that in consumer insurance "basis of the contract" clauses, whether in the proposal form or the contract itself, should be ineffective to make all the answers given by the insured into warranties. (This is without prejudice to the decision whether or not to permit specific warranties of existing fact contained within the contract.)

OTHER ISSUES

Material Available to Insurers

In many cases information which is relevant to an insurance application or renewal will be held by the insurer or be readily available to it. In this section we consider the extent to which insurers should retain their rights in respect of misrepresentation if they fail to make their own enquiries. The FOS has put the point to us in the following terms: There are issues of good faith in the practice of declining to seek information at the application stage of an insurance policy in the full knowledge that this information will be sought in the event of a claim. The effect of such practice is that information that is supposed to be provided in order for the underwriter to assess the risk and to decide upon the terms of the policy is only in fact being requested from the insured in order to see if the claim can be rejected. We have identified three types of situation where these issues arise – where data is readily available to an insurer, where data is held in the insurer's own files and where the insurer has obtained consent from the policyholder to obtain the data but has not done so.

Our tentative proposals apply only to those cases where the misrepresentation by the insured was nonfraudulent.

Data Readily Available to Insurers

The National Consumer Council has argued that law established in respect of contracts between merchants in the eighteenth century is not necessarily appropriate to consumer contracts in the modern environment. In particular, it is clear that the balance of knowledge has changed: It is generally accepted, too, that the balance between insurance seller and insurance consumer has altered since 1766, to put the seller in a far stronger position when it comes to assessing risk. The sophisticated data available to insurance companies through the Association of British Insurers and their own company intelligence is not available to individual consumers.

As the NCC has noted, insurers may have access to relevant information through various databases. Again there is no general obligation on insurers to check these databases at the time of an application, midterm adjustment or renewal.

One example is the Claims and Underwriting Exchange "CUE", which is a database of incidents reported to subscribing insurers and which may provide a more accurate record of past claims and losses than policyholders can give from memory. 24 Another example is information about flood risks, We think it may not be unreasonable for a consumer to assume that the insurer will be wellinformed of the known risk in the particular area.

In discussions a number of points have been made to us about the use of such databases:

(1) The information obtained will not necessarily be complete, uptodate or accurate. CUE, for example, relies on other insurers submitting accurate information in a prompt manner.

(2) There is typically a cost in searching such databases – both in terms of the time involved and any access charge that is payable. This cost is likely to be passed on to policyholders.

(3) Subscription to any given database is not compulsory. If subscribers could be penalised for failing to carry out searches, one respondent asked: "Would this lead to different standards being applied to insurers that subscribed to such databases and those that do not?".

(4) Some of the databases are subject to significant restrictions. CUE, for example, only covers certain classes of insurance.

Nevertheless the fact remains that some insurers are avoiding policies and rejecting claims on the basis of facts which could have been readily established at outset. In his Pat Saxton Memorial Lecture, Lord Justice Longmore suggested a test that we think may be appropriate: whether the undisclosed matter was a matter which a reasonable insured would realise was within the knowledge only of himself (or those for whom he is responsible) rather than a matter which could have been independently investigated and verified by insurers. This addresses nondisclosure but the same principle should apply to incomplete answers in response to questions, if the insured reasonably thought that the insurer would investigate and verify the matter.

We tentatively propose that an insurer should not be allowed to rely on a failure to disclose or a misrepresentation because of an incomplete answer, if the insured reasonably thought that the insurer would investigate and verify the matter.

Data in the Insurer's Own Files

Insurers may hold relevant information in their records for example, information relating to another policy held by the same consumer.

However, there is currently no general obligation on them to carry out searches at application or renewal if they have no reason to believe anything material might be found. Professor Clarke has suggested that other jurisdictions have a better rule: In the United States and in Canada, if insurers fail to look in their data files, they are deemed to have waived disclosure of the information which the files contain. So should it be in England today.

We appreciate that there are practical difficulties which may face an insurer. Information may be held in different forms – paper files, microfiche, computer records, and so on. It may be held across different sites, and by different companies within the same group.

Nevertheless, if the information was reasonably identifiable we believe that the insurer should not retain its rights in misrepresentation if it has failed to make the necessary enquiries.

We tentatively propose that an insurer should be treated as knowing information contained in its own files, provided that the information was reasonably identifiable.

Data Insurer has Asked Permission to Obtain

The problem is compounded if the insurer chooses not to obtain information from a third party after obtaining a consumer's consent to do so. The consumer is very likely to assume that this information will be obtained by the insurer from the third party and thus that the consumer does not need to disclose it themselves. For example, a life insurance application form may authorise an insurer to obtain medical details from the consumer's general practitioner, but there is no obligation on the insurer to make use of this authorisation.

In 1993, Dr Julian Farrand, then Insurance Ombudsman, drew attention to the confusion this can cause:...the reasonable expectation of the ordinary policyholder for life assurance would surely be that, where the details of a doctor are asked for, he would be approached by the assurer and would supply all relevant details before the proposal could be accepted... Indeed, many people wonder why assurers ask for such details if they only intend to use them if a claim is made. By underwriting the risk without carrying out full enquiries at the underwriting stage, the assurer lulls the policyholder into a false sense of security that he has cover when the reality is that he has none because as soon as a claim is made, the assurer will write to his doctor and discover the information then said to be material. If it is that material, it should have been investigated earlier and the risk declined or a higher premium charged, or cover restricted.

We tentatively propose that an insurer who has indicated that it may obtain information from a third party (by for example asking the insured for consent to obtain it) should not be allowed to rely on a nonfraudulent misrepresentation (or failure to disclose) if the insured reasonably thought that the insurer would check with the third party.

We note with interest that the Application Form Design for Life and Health Protection Insurances ("AFD") suggests two optional warnings that may be included on application forms: Even where these warnings are used, there are likely to be situations where a policyholder reasonably thinks that the insurer will have contacted their doctor. Failure to follow up incomplete or inconsistent answers

On occasion an applicant for insurance will either fail to answer a question or give an answer which is incomplete or inconsistent. The issue then arises – if the insurer fails to make further enquiries, has it waived its right to disclosure of the missing information?

In some cases, failure to answer a question may to a reasonable person appear to be an answer in itself. In *Roberts v Avon Insurance Company Limited* 29 the applicant was asked to complete the following declaration which contained a blank space: I have suffered no similar loss, except... It was held that a failure to fill in the blank space was in itself a definitive answer that there had been no similar losses.

There could be no question of the insurer having waived disclosure of the relevant information.

Where an answer is incomplete, the issue is whether the incompleteness should have been apparent. If it should have been apparent then the insurer may have waived its right to disclosure if it makes no further enquiries.

An applicant may give answers which seem to conflict. For example, in *Winter v Irish Life Assurance plc,* 30 the consumer stated incorrectly that she was suffering from no illness, but disclosed that as a child she had suffered from meconium ileus – a precursor to cystic fibrosis. It was held that the insurer was not obliged to investigate the potential conflict between these answers.

Australia has a provision which precludes an insurer from raising an allegation of nondisclosure or misrepresentation when a question in a proposal form has not been answered or has an obviously incomplete answer. 31 The onus is on the insurer to follow up such a form as soon as it is received. We think a similar rule might usefully be introduced here.

We tentatively propose that insurers should be precluded from relying on a nondisclosure or misrepresentation when a question in a proposal form that requires an answer has not been answered or has an obviously incomplete answer.
A cutoff period

This option is relevant to longterm insurance business. There is a particular risk if the policy can be avoided when the claim is made since the insured may well have relied on the policy to provide essential financial protection for innocent third party dependants.

Moreover, by that stage it may be very hard for the insured or their dependants to prove what was or was not said at the time the proposal was completed. Should the insurer be able to raise issues of misrepresentation that it could have raised when or soon after the policy was taken out?

It is worth canvassing a 'cutoff' period for defences other than fraud. In essence, the insurer would be prevented from relying on any misrepresentation or nondisclosure at the application stage once the policy had been in force for a set number of years say 3 or 5. The attraction of such a provision is that insurers would be encouraged to find out all they need to know as early as possible.

This is the approach taken in New Zealand. Under section 4 of the Insurance Law Reform Act 1977, life insurers may not avoid for a misrepresentation unless the statement, was substantially incorrect material and Was made either—

(i) Fraudulently or

(ii) Within the period of 3 years immediately preceding the date on which the policy is sought to be avoided or the date of the death of the life insured, whichever is the earlier.

One option would be to apply a similar rule to consumer life insurance, and we would welcome views on its advantages and disadvantages.

We ask whether in consumer life assurance the insurer should be prevented from relying on any nonfraudulent misrepresentation after the policy has been in force for three years.

7

BUSINESS INSURANCE CONTRACTS

INTRODUCTION

The 1980 Report took the view that the problems with insurance law are not confined to the consumer market. The BILA Report and Lord Justice Longmore's lecture were also concerned to see reform of the law governing business insurance. In this Part we discuss whether there is a need to reform the law as it applies to insurance taken out by businesses. We start by considering insurance for business generally. At the end of the Part we consider, in turn, Marine Aviation and Transport insurance ("MAT"), reinsurance and insurance for small businesses.

The principal question must be whether the four major changes that we have tentatively put forward for consumer insurance should apply to business insurance also. It would obviously be simpler, and would avoid awkward "boundary disputes", if the same rules were applied to all types of insurance.

However we recognise that differences in the markets may make this impractical or undesirable~ or that the practical importance of the issues we deal with may be so slight that reform of business insurance contract law is simply "not worth the candle."

It should be noted that the jurisdictions examined for the paper treat businesses the same as consumers. Any differences apply as between marine and nonmarine insurance, in the case of France, Australia and New York. The jurisdictions also differentiate between normal insurance and reinsurance.

We would welcome views from all sides of industry on whether the issues we identify below cause problems in practice. We also want to know if they have an impact on the market – and in particular whether they have a positive or negative impact on the competitiveness of insurance policies written under English or Scots law.

GENERAL ISSUES

We begin with some general points before we turn to the individual points. Most businesses are not insurance experts

Although almost all businesses need to buy insurance, for most it is ancillary to their main trade. As the 1980 report said: There are certain mischiefs in the law of nondisclosure which apply equally whether the insured is a consumer or a businessman who is not constantly concerned in his business activities with the insurance market.

Neither consumers nor ordinary businessmen who are not in the insurance market have the knowledge or experience to identify all facts which may be material to insurers. Both are therefore to this extent in need of protection and both may properly be regarded as consumers visàvis insurers.

The British Insurance Law Association also stressed this point: "a tradesman insuring his business is in as much need of protection as when he is insuring his home". Lord Justice Longmore argued that the fact the insurance industry accepts that the strict law needs to be modified for consumers suggests strongly that it should also be modified for businesses: How can it be right that a lawyer insuring his home and household possession can rely on the more relaxed test of nondisclosure under the Statements of Practice, but the small trader, eg the garage owner or the fishmonger insuring his premises, cannot?

In 1980, the English Law Commission pointed to harsh cases involving small businesses, especially where the nondisclosed issue related to moral hazard. For example, in *Locker & Woolf Ltd v Western Australian Insurance Co*, a fire claim was rejected on the grounds that the applicant had not revealed that the partnership had previously been refused motor cover.

We do not think that many people running noninsurance businesses would understand the full extent of the duty of disclosure that the law requires. They are unlikely to understand, for example, that they must volunteer information about criminal offences their employees have committed, 4 or any previous rejection for insurance. Brokers or inhouse expertise

That said, many applicants will be advised by brokers, and some may have specialist staff. This is sometimes also true for consumers, but with business insurance it is much more common.

In our Scoping Paper we drew attention to the type of problem that can arise where an applicant for insurance discloses material facts to an intermediary and the intermediary fails to pass on that information to the insurer. We intend to address this issue in a later paper – it does not form part of current discussions.

More generally we do not think that the involvement of an intermediary should affect the test of materiality, though it may affect the standard of disclosure that can be expected from an insured.

Supporting Trust and Confidence in the Market

Even for large commercial risks, the insurance market is built on trust and generally accepted standards of market practice. We are concerned that the law undercuts rather than supports accepted market practice.

Let us take the example of avoidance. Avoidance is an appropriate remedy for conduct involving some form of dishonesty, but the law allows it to be used where an insured has acted innocently or inadvertently in making an untrue statement or failing to disclose a fact that is known to be material.

Insurance solicitors dealing with high value claims justify the current law on the ground that it is necessary to prevent sharp dealing. As one solicitor put it: Time and again [nondisclosure] isn't inadvertent. A commercial decision has been made: this will not be insured if we tell the whole truth. And in those circumstances the sanction [of avoidance] should remain.

It is often said that the full remedy of avoidance will only be applied if there is some element of fraud or dishonesty. We were told that good market practice is that an insurer will honour an insurance contract unless there is some element of dishonesty on the part of the insured.

I always advise my clients that if they get a whiff of nondisclosure or misrepresentation, basically the panel or court has to think there is a bit of a stitchup here. You don't really avoid for technical nondisclosure.

However, if the law permits insurers to avoid for purely technical nondisclosure, it is inevitable that some insurers will take the point. When we asked one firm whether insurers would ever attempt to avoid a policy for an innocent nondisclosure, this is the answer we received: Some would, especially in a climate where money is tight. I suspect that they still would. Yes. And what also there is the potential for with the big commercial [risks]... they're subscribed to by three, five, twenty different insurers. And you could have three or four who are perhaps looking at insolvency problems or whatever and will in truth seize on any opportunity they can. So... to take comfort in the thought that the market as a whole will not take the point on innocent disclosure–you might be surprised really. There would be a risk that some parts of it would. When we asked whether that particular firm would attempt to avoid for an innocent nondisclosure, we were told that they would if instructed to: That is the current law, so we would, yes... We wouldn't really have a choice.

If the insured had indeed acted fraudulently, we need have little sympathy. However, if the law provides insurers with a strong financial incentive to attempt to avoid even where there was no fraud, it is inevitable that some insurers in some circumstances will use the weapon they have been given. This has the potential to undercut more ethical insurers and to undermine confidence in the UK market. It can contribute to the perception that the law in this country is unduly insurerfriendly.

The Insurer is Judge and Jury

A particular complaint is that while reputable insurers will not avoid for innocent misrepresentation or nondisclosure, they may do so if they suspect fraud, even if they cannot prove it. This effectively allows them to be "judge and jury in their own cause". In other contexts the courts have roundly condemned provisions that, in effect, oust their jurisdiction.

All or Nothing Remedies

Under the current law, an insurer may avoid whenever it can show that, had it known the information, it would only have altered a single term of the contract, a term which need not have any connection with the disputed claim. Moreover, the current law, does not permit half measures. An insurer cannot pay a claim and avoid for the future, or accept liability for a proportion of the claim. It must either seek to avoid completely, or waive all rights to a remedy. As one solicitor put it: There are avoidance cases where... you have to say to the [insurer] client, I'm sorry, you've got one remedy, and the client may say – 'that's very heavy – we don't particularly want to go that far'... If they don't, they lose the remedy completely. So it's pay or avoid... It means [the insurers] have to avoid or abandon their right. And they have shareholders and people.

Even in cases where it seems right to allow an insurer some remedy, avoidance can appear to be excessively harsh. Lord Justice Longmore makes this point, quoting *Kausar v Eagle Star*: Avoidance for nondisclosure is a drastic remedy. It enables the insurer to disclaim liability after, and not before, he has discovered that the risk turns out to be a bad one~ it leaves the insurer without the protection which he thought he had contracted and paid for... I do consider that there should be some restraint in the operation of the doctrine.

In practice, of course, most cases are resolved through some sort of settlement. The insurer alleges nondisclosure and misrepresentation~ the insured denies that the fact is material, or pleads that it was a mere expectation or belief, held in good faith. After some horsetrading, a settlement is reached. Lawyers acting for insurers worried that if the law was changed to provide proportional remedies the insurer would have to start by offering more, and would end up paying more: Instead of going into negotiations saying we are paying nothing and end up paying half, we would say we would pay a third and end up paying two thirds. Inevitably, most cases will be resolved through bargaining conducted in the shadow of the legal rules. Our concern is that the current legal rules have little connection to fairness or market expectations, but instead provide insurers with a weapon that can be wielded simply to reduce the size of a settlement.

Pooling of Risks

It is frequently said that the law is too much in favour of the insurer, and that it needs to be rebalanced in favour of the insured. We think that the question of balance between insurer and insured is one that must be approached with great care.

In our view the question is not really whether the law favours one or other party too much. It is whether the rules that will be applied when the parties have not made a different agreement (for example, have not agreed that the insurer may not avoid for innocent misrepresentation) represent a fair or efficient balance. To put it another way, had both parties known of the potential issue in advance, what would they have agreed?

To the best of our knowledge, the insurance market is fully competitive in terms of price. Putting it simply, the insured gets what it pays for. If the law is to be changed so as to give the insured more rights for example, by preventing the insurer from avoiding the contract on the ground of an innocent misrepresentation or nondisclosure, there will be a marginal increase in the cost of policies, since insurers will now be obliged to pay out on some policies that under the old law they might have avoided. However, whether the market is less competitive depends on the preferences of insureds. If it is true that insurers will normally pay in such a case unless there is a suggestion of fraud, and that fraud is rare, the increase is likely to be low. While some insureds may prefer to pay slightly less and take the risk that their policy is avoided because of a purely innocent, nonnegligent misrepresentation on their part, others may prefer to pay a slightly higher premium to have this risk transferred to the pool of risks covered by the insurer.

The Parties are Free to Agree what they Want

An argument often made against reform is that it is unnecessary because the current law is not compulsory~ if insureds don't like it, they can ask for better terms in their policy. In other words, the market will take care of any problem without the need for reform.

No doubt there are insureds who are sufficiently sophisticated to study very carefully the terms offered by potential insurers and who bargain for changes in their favour. It is quite clear from the cases and from the many sad histories supplied to us that there are large numbers of business insureds who do not. They may have no expertise in insurance law and may simply not be able to understand the effect of the policy offered. They may not be able to afford expert advice or may rationally take the view that the chances of a problem occurring are low enough that it is not worthwhile to spend time or money doing so. If they are not important customers, then even if they are aware of the difficulties they may be unable to persuade the insurer to write a special policy just for them. That is a quite understandable reaction on the part of the insurer, since for many types of relatively lowvalue insurance, writing and administering policies on different terms may be uneconomic. But whatever the reason, if the insured would in fact have been willing to pay a sufficient additional premium to cover the cost of the improvement in cover plus the regular profit element, there is a form of market failure – the terms of the contract are inefficient.

Thus the question is whether the rules for business insurance can be made to correspond more closely to what insureds want – and, given the generally high standards of the vast majority of insurers, insureds probably think that they are getting when they buy insurance in the UK market.

Mandatory or Default Rules

The rules we have proposed for consumer insurance would be mandatory rules to the extent that the parties would not be free to vary them in favour of the insurer. We need to consider whether whatever rules are thought appropriate for business insurance should be similarly mandatory, should be merely default rules that the parties are free to vary or should be semimandatory in the sense that they can be varied provided that the change from the default rules is "fair". (That is the test applied to consumer contracts in general, though not to the 'core terms', under Unfair Terms in Consumer Contracts Regulations 1999.)

In general terms we do not favour mandatory rules for business insurance contracts. We think it is important to preserve freedom of contract unless there is a very good reason to depart from it. Nor do we favour applying a fairness test, except perhaps for insurance contracts with small businesses. 8 The reason is quite simply the uncertainty that such controls can create. Thus we think that for business insurance contracts in general, any proposed rules should be default rules that can be disapplied by contrary agreement.

It may be argued that this will defeat the object of reform insurers will simply write their contracts to reflect the old law. Most insurance contracts are on standard terms~ all we would be achieving would be an alteration in the standard terms.

We do not think that this is true, nor that, if it were, it would necessarily follow that reform is pointless. First, we think most insurers would be reluctant to reduce the rights of the insured from the legal norm without discussing the matter expressly with the insured.

Most insurers are rightly proud of their reputation and it would do their reputation no good at all to be found to have taken away the insured's "new rights" by means of a standard term that was not expressly agreed by the parties. And of course if the parties do freely agree to revert to the position under the old law, there can be no objection. That is what freedom of contract means.

Secondly, having to insert special terms to revert to the previous position at least gives the insured a chance to discover what is happening by reading the terms. If they object, they can then try to bargain for something better. Indeed, we hope that the publicity that would inevitably surround any change in the law of insurance would positively encourage insureds to ask insurers: are my rights under the new Insurance Act fully protected?

Lastly, insurers may be reluctant to try to reduce the insured's rights by means of standard clauses for fear that they may not work. It has to be remembered that the courts will interpret the terms of the insurance contract, when there is doubt, in favour of the insured (under the contra proferentem rule) but they will do so against the background of the existing law.

In other words, if a provision merely leaves in place the insurer's current rights, it is unlikely to be given a narrow interpretation. But were the law to be changed to give the insured more rights, a clause excluding those rights would probably be read narrowly. The insurer would have to use very clear words. We do not think this would be inappropriate. The parties should be free to agree what they want but insureds should be left in no doubt where they stand.

Keeping UK Law Competitive

The insurance industry makes a significant contribution to the invisible earnings of the UK. However, we have been told that in recent years the London market in particular has lost a large amount of international business, and that this has been partly as a result of the state of insurance contract law.

It has been suggested that from the perspective of brokers or policyholders, other jurisdictions provide a more attractive legal regime. Bermuda, France and Norway are amongst the countries mentioned.

To date, definitive figures on the loss of business have proved elusive. Furthermore, one observer suggested that the loss was a positive development: Yes, we've lost 40% of the business but it was the 40% we wanted to lose!

Nevertheless, we would like to explore how reforms in the law might support the UK insurance industry and therefore invite views on this issue.

It is our tentative proposal that the law affecting business insurance should be changed to give the insured certain additional rights, but that the rules should in general not be mandatory.

NONDISCLOSURE

In Part 6 we tentatively proposed that consumers should no longer have a residual duty of disclosure. 9 Rather, insurers should have to ask for the information they need. They should be entitled to ask questions in general terms ("Are there any other facts that we ought to know?") but the answers given should be judged by what the reasonable consumer would think was being asked about. Thus if the consumer reasonably thought that a fact they did not reveal was not material, the insurer would have no remedy.

Should the same apply to business insurance? Although there is no such duty in several of the jurisdictions that compete with the UK (such as New York), our tentative view is that it would not be right to abolish the residual duty of disclosure for businesses. There are two reasons for this.

First, the duty of disclosure has become part of the way the UK business insurance market works. For many business policies, there is no proposal form. Instead the broker presents the risk, and the underwriter relies on the broker and client to present that risk honestly. It would be possible to distinguish insurance that was preceded by a proposal form (whether a paper form or on a website) and insurance where there was no such form, and require disclosure only in the latter. However we would prefer, if possible, not to set arbitrary boundaries between types of insurance. These always cause problems in marginal cases.

Secondly, we think that business insurance in general is probably subject to a much greater variety of risks than is consumer insurance. That would make it much harder for the insurer to ask questions about all the relevant risks.

Thirdly, while not all business insurance is done through intermediaries who can advise as to what is required, a far greater proportion of it is. This means that the risk of an insured not realising that it has a general duty to disclose is reduced.

We still think that it would be appropriate to expect insurers, as a matter of good practice, to warn insureds about the duty to disclose when it is reasonable to think that the insured may not be aware of the need, particularly on renewal. This might well be the case with many kinds of business insurance written on an annual basis. But we doubt it is necessary to provide a legal remedy, such as preventing the insurer from avoiding, for failure to do so.

We tentatively propose that the duty of disclosure should continue to apply to business insurance contracts in general.

REDEFINING MATERIALITY

Different Degrees of Sophistication

In 1980, the Law Commission recommended reform not just for consumers but for all insureds outside the marine, aviation and transport markets. Although the gap between what an underwriter understands to be material and what a policyholder understands to be material is greatest for consumers, the injustice is not confined to consumer policies. Small and medium businesses may also have little understanding of insurance, and in some cases will be less protected than are consumers. As we have seen, small businesses make relatively little use of the Financial Ombudsman Scheme. Even if a small business does use the scheme, the Statements of Practice will not necessarily be applied~ so only some will be granted consumerstyle protection. Medium businesses with a turnover of £1 million or more do not have the right to use an ombudsman at all.

Overdisclosure

There is even an argument that the current law operates against the interests of insurers in that they get too much information when the insured is sophisticated.

The duty of disclosure is so wide and, to many insureds, so imprecise that an insured may conclude that the safest option is to give the insurer all the information it is able to gather. We have been told that applicants often provide insurers with more information than they are able to process. As one experienced insurance lawyer put it: We are now at the stage where commercial brokers are tending to walk into underwriters with three CDs and tell them, 'it's all in there'.

We were told, for example, about a South American highways authority that provided the insurer with a survey report on each road, in Spanish: "It took us 2 weeks to get it translated". With the development of information technology, the problem is likely to increase.

To some extent, if the parties have the ability to transmit large quantities of information, they will. However, we think that a narrower test of what is material just might do less to encourage the present tendency to inundate the insurer with information.

Modify the Duty

Our tentative view is that the ambit of the duty of disclosure should be modified in business cases, to include only what a reasonable insured in the circumstances would understand to be material to the underwriter in question. We think this test is sufficiently flexible to adapt to the many different circumstances in which insurance is used and sold. The same test should apply in cases of misrepresentation.

In many insurance markets, in particular where both parties are knowledgeable about insurance and what is likely to be relevant, the effect of this change would be minimal. One advantage of a "reasonable insured test" is that it is flexible enough to cope with a variety of policyholders. In the more sophisticated markets, where both insurers and insured are professionally represented, we would expect almost no difference between what a reasonable insurer and a reasonable insured would regard as material. Here the two tests are effectively synonymous. As the gap between the two sides grows, so does the effect of the reform. A reasonable insured test has the advantage that it does not require legislators to define arbitrary lines by, for example, distinguishing businesses by their size or level of sophistication. As the British Insurance Law

Association put it in their 2002 report, the test would enable the court to differentiate between the duty of a large industrial company with a professional insurance department, as compared with a small company on an industrial estate where the insured's knowledge of insurance law may well be very limited.

In assessing what a reasonable insured in the circumstances would understand to be material to the underwriter in question, a court could also take into account whether the policyholder had received professional advice from an intermediary.

The Nature of the Evidence

We have been told that there are advantages in the present "prudent underwriter" test, because the issue of what underwriters think is material may be determined by expert evidence from the industry. Solicitors acting for insurers can locate expert underwriters and ask them to give evidence in court. They expressed concern that a reasonable insured test was inherently uncertain. In the absence of any recognised "reasonable insureds" to give evidence, they thought it would merely invite the judge to substitute his or her own opinion for that of the industry.

In 1980, the Law Commission saw the prominence granted to insurers' evidence as a serious criticism of the current law: Such evidence will usually be readily available to the insurers, who will have no difficulty in selecting appropriate witnesses. However the insured will often be at a considerable disadvantage in finding expert witnesses prepared to challenge those of the insurer and the position of such witnesses is often invidious. Some judicial doubt has also been cast on the cogency of such evidence.

Under our proposed reform, the actual insurer in question will need to start by showing that the issue was material to them, in that if they had known the truth they would not have entered into the same contract on the same terms.

The judge or arbitrator would then need to determine what the reasonable insured would have understood to be material in the circumstances. We expect that in many cases involving small businesses, judges would indeed draw on their own understanding to ask how a reasonable small business would regard the matter.

However, in more specialist markets, there will still be a need for expert evidence. Where the parties are relying on established practice in the market, we anticipate that this evidence may be given by a range of experienced professionals, including insureds, brokers or underwriters.

Thus for generalist markets, judges could be expected to draw on their own understanding of what a reasonable small business would understand to be material. For specialist markets, evidence about what is reasonable may be given by a range of experienced professionals.

An alternative would be to take up a suggestion we made in relation to consumer insurance. This is that a revised test of materiality might ask whether a reasonable insurer with the same knowledge of the client would expect the insured to understand that a particular matter was relevant. That would once more be a question on which the court might hear evidence from underwriters and brokers.

Conclusion on Materiality

We tentatively propose that a reasonable insured test of materiality should apply to all business insurance.

This would be a default rather than a mandatory rule of law. In other words, the parties will be free to agree a different test by means of an explicit term in the contract.

12 However, the need to obtain agreement to a different test will, we hope, serve the useful purpose of alerting a prospective policyholder to the importance of the issue. It will then, of course, then be open to that prospective policyholder to ask the insurer to explain exactly what information is required.

DISTINGUISHING BETWEEN FRAUDULENT, INNOCENT AND NEGLIGENT CONDUCT

In Part 6 we distinguish between behaviour that is fraudulent, innocent but negligent, and innocent without negligence. We tentatively conclude that for consumer insurance, avoidance is appropriate where the insured has behaved fraudulently. Where the insured has behaved innocently and reasonably, insurers should take policyholders as they find them. Where the insured has behaved negligently, the law should as far as possible put the parties into the position they would have been in had the facts been stated correctly.

Here we consider whether the same rules should be applied to businesses, or whether there are reasons to treat business insurance differently. We think that there is no case for restricting the insurer's right to avoid the policy (and therefore to refuse to pay any claim) where a business insured has behaved fraudulently. Below we discuss three more difficult issues:

(1) Should the insurer be entitled to a remedy where the insured has behaved innocently and not negligently?

(2) Where the insured has behaved negligently but not fraudulently, should the insurer be granted a proportionate remedy?

(3) Where should the balance of proving fraud lie?

If a proportionate remedy is to be applied, we then consider two ancillary issues: how should the law treat cases where the insurer should have declined the risk~ and what rights should an insurer have to avoid in the future.

Innocent Misrepresentation or Nondisclosure

The first question is whether there should continue to be a legal right to avoid for innocent nonnegligent misrepresentation or nondisclosure.

We have already discussed this in relation to the general issues of trust in the market and the pooling of risks, and it seems unnecessary to repeat what was said there. The basic question is whether in general insureds would prefer to pay the slight increase in premiums that might be involved as the price for knowing that no policy can be avoided for nonnegligent misrepresentation by the insured.

We have considered where the burden of proof should lie. We think that the information available to the insured when it made the misrepresentation or failed to make the disclosure will normally be a matter largely within its own knowledge.

We think it is useful to draw the analogy with Misrepresentation Act 1967, section 2(1), and place the burden of disproving fraud or negligence on the insured. The Act provides (in effect) that when a misrepresentation has been made, the misrepresentee can recover damages for any resulting loss unless the misrepresentor can prove that, up until the time the contract was made, it had reasonable grounds to believe and did believe that the statement it made was true.

We tentatively propose that when a business insured has acted without negligence in making an incorrect statement or in other ways (such as failing to answer a question), the insurer should have no right to avoid the policy or to refuse to pay a claim under it on that ground.

Negligence: a Proportionate Remedy?

In Part 6 we reach the tentative conclusion that where a consumer proposer has made a negligent misrepresentation, the court should apply a proportionate remedy by asking what the insurer would have done had it known the true facts. In particular:

(1) where an insurer would have excluded a particular type of claim, the insurer should not be obliged to pay claims that would not fall within the exclusion

(2) where an insurer would have declined the risk altogether, the claim may be refused~

(3) where an insurer would have charged more, the claim should be reduced proportionately to the underpayment of premium.

Many insurance lawyers accept the theory behind these proposals. The main concern is how the issues would be determined in practice. Solicitors expressed concern that each side would bring experts to contradict what the other side said: Each side will have an expert each, which will say the opposite of the other. It's not as if they all have rating books and tariffs... In France, for example, there are fixed tariffs. What would actually happen at the box is that we would propose a premium, and the broker would say, 'Oh, that's a bit steep. Charlie down the road does it for half that.' And they would end up with a number without any science at all.

The problems are likely to be greater in relation to business insurance than they would be for consumer insurance. But we do not see them as insuperable. However unscientific the negotiations may be, they would be a more accurate assessment of the loss involved than the current law, which permits unscrupulous insurers to wield a dominant weapon.

A more difficult question is whether in business insurance, where the average insured is far more likely to be aware of what it should be doing, it is desirable to create stronger incentives.

This was the reason given for refusing to apply the discretion to refuse rescission under Misrepresentation Act 1967 section 2(2) to contracts of insurance. If business insureds know that if they make a careless mistake they will not recover anything under the policy, they would have a stronger incentive to be careful. Conversely, insureds may be willing to carry the small increase in premiums necessary to cover the cost of "innocent mistakes" as one of the pooled risks, but may feel very differently about sharing the costs of other people's negligence.

We welcome views on whether the remedy for negligent misrepresentation should be proportionate, in that it should aim to put the insurer into the position it would have been in had it known the true circumstances.

Proving Fraud

We are conscious that this approach would mean that the insurer would only have an incontestable right to avoid the policy and refuse to pay the claim if it could prove fraud, and that fraud is hard to prove. Where the insured is a company, in particular, it can be extremely difficult to pin down who knew what at which stage, or to impute knowledge to the controlling mind of the organisation. We do not wish to give an advantage to organisations that fail to investigate safety issues properly, or where the directors isolate themselves from matters they should have known about.

We think that these concerns could be eased by two presumptions:

(1) that an insured knew what a person in their position would be expected to know~ and

(2) that if the insurer asked a clear question about the matter, the insured knew that any inaccuracy in their answer was material.

The first presumption is similar to section 18(1) of the Marine Insurance Act 1906, whereby the insured is "deemed to know every circumstance which, in the ordinary course of business, ought to be known by him".

Unlike section 18(1), however, it would be rebuttable. The insured would be able to bring evidence that they did not know the facts, even though they should. However, the burden of proving this would be on the insured. Similarly, if the insured did not think a question was material, it would have to show why not.

We ask whether the insured should have to show that it did not know what a person in its position would be expected to know, or alternatively that it did not know why an inaccurate response to a clear question was material.

Further Issues

If it is decided that proportionality should be applied where appropriate, two further questions arise.

Cases where Another Insurer would have Accepted the Risk

For consumers we also asked whether the courts should have an additional discretion. We suggested this may apply where the insurer would have declined the risk, but the policyholder's fault is minor, and other insurers would have accepted the risk at a higher premium.

This may also apply where the misrepresented fact is unrelated to the claim. On balance, we think that such a discretion is more appropriate to consumers than to businesses, but we would welcome advice on the issue.

We ask whether where the insurer would have declined the risk, but the policyholder's fault is minor and other insurers would have accepted the risk at a higher premium, the court should have a discretion to apply a proportionality solution.

Avoidance for the Future

We also asked whether insurers should be entitled to cancel policies for the future in all cases, or only where they would have declined the risk. We noted that the FOS would sometimes require insurers to amend the terms of a policy, and abide by it in the future. Again, we think this may be appropriate only in consumer cases. Our starting point in business cases is that where the insured has made a negligent misrepresentation or nondisclosure, even if the insurer should have to pay a proportion of the claim in question, it should be entitled to cancel the policy for the future. We would expect the insurer to give reasonable notice and return a proportionate part of the premium.

We tentatively propose that negligent misrepresentation or nondisclosure should be a ground on which the insurer may cancel the policy after reasonable notice, without prejudice to claims that have arisen or arise within the notice period.

BASIS OF THE CONTRACT CLAUSES

In Part 6 we propose to abolish basis of the contract clauses in consumer cases. These have been criticised for many years and their use has been outlawed in Australia and New Zealand. We think we would need to enact something along similar lines to prevent evasion of our other proposals.

We think that basis of the contract clauses should be abolished in business contracts, for the same reasons. There would need at least to be a provision that incorrect answers would not give rise to a remedy for breach of warranty unless there was a term to that effect in the contract itself, rather than merely a "basis of the contract" clause in the proposal form. This is a rule that would have to be mandatory, otherwise the mere insertion of a basis of the contract clause might be taken as a 'contracting out' from all the rules proposed in this section.

We tentatively propose that there should be a mandatory rule that incorrect answers would not give rise to a remedy for breach of warranty unless there was a term to that effect in the contract itself, rather than merely a "basis of the contract" clause in the proposal form.

MARINE, AVIATION AND TRANSPORT INSURANCE

The 1980 report excluded MAT insurance from the scope of its reforms. It argued that the people working in this market were generally professionals "who could reasonably be expected to be aware of the niceties of insurance law". 14 The law was certain and understood, and worked satisfactorily.

However, the Commission accepted that the line between MAT and other insurance was not a clear one, and that some individuals with pleasure craft did need additional protection. The Commission expressed unease with the definitions of MAT used in previous regulations, and suggested some omissions. It also proposed that the Secretary of State should be empowered to vary the definition by regulation.

Here we are not minded to make a distinction between MAT and other forms of insurance, for three reasons.

(1) We are told MAT is no longer regarded as such a separate and distinct form of insurance.

(2) It would be overly complex to require lawyers to apply one law to (for example) major constructions, and quite a different law to ships.

(3) The boundary between MAT and other insurance is extremely difficult to draft. We would not only need to extend protection to consumers who own pleasure craft but also many small leisure businesses and fishermen. The result would be complex regulations, with arbitrary dividing lines.

(4) The difference between full avoidance and a proportional remedy is greatest in the very largest claims, where several million pounds may be at stake. With such large claims, the result of insurance litigation is likely to affect the solvency of the firm, and therefore have knock on consequences not only for shareholders but also for creditors, employees and third party claimants. Even in large sophisticated businesses, information does not always get passed on in the way it should, and the consequences may be borne by people who are not sophisticated at all. There is still a need for the law to reflect accepted notions of fairness and good market practice.

We tentatively propose that our earlier proposals for business insurance should apply to MAT.

THIRD PARTY CLAIMS

It has been suggested to us that proportionality produces an unsatisfactory result where the claim in question relates to the policyholder's liability to a third party. The point in question is whether it is desirable that the rights of a third party are affected by the acts or omissions of the policyholder.

Under the Road Traffic Act 1988 an insurer is obliged to meet thirdparty claims in motor insurance cases, even where a policy has been avoided for misrepresentation or nondisclosure by the policyholder. 15 For most lines of business there is no such protection the third party will have rights only against the policyholder.

If the policyholder is insolvent, the third party can bring a claim direct against the insurer under the Third Parties (Rights against Insurers) Act 1930. 16 However, defences such as misrepresentation or nondisclosure which are available to the insurer against the policyholder can, however, also be used against a third party.

We can see that there may be arguments for giving third parties Road Traffic Act style protection – particularly where insurance is compulsory under statute, contract or professional rules. For example, a professional may be obliged to effect professional indemnity insurance. Such insurance is intended to provide compensation for third parties clients affected by the professional's negligence. However, we suspect that even in such cases the matter is best left to the relevant professional body. It can decide first whether such insurance should be compulsory and second the terms on which it should be written, which might including modifying the rights of an insurer to rely on misrepresentation or nondisclosure. In doing so, it can take into account the availability or otherwise of such cover in the insurance market.

Our tentative conclusion, therefore, is that we should not extend the existing rights of third parties, but we welcome views on this issue.

REINSURANCE

Our starting point is the principle that the same rules should apply to reinsurance as to insurance unless a good case is made for distinguishing between the two.

We recognise that there are important practical differences between the ways in which insurance and reinsurance are conducted. A member of our Advisory Panel suggested that three matters in particular should be considered:

(1) Much reinsurance is placed under obligatory treaties. If a risk falls within the terms agreed, the insurer is obliged to place it under the treaty and the reinsurer is bound to accept it. Disclosure of the details of individual risks is not typically required.

(2) Facultative business coming in to the London market from abroad is frequently written on a fronting basis, so that the local insurer is simply the conduit for passing the risk to reinsurers. In that situation, the majority of material facts will relate not to the reinsurance itself but to the underlying risk which will have been written under a contract governed by a foreign law with its own disclosure rules.

(3) The parties entering into reinsurance agreements are both conducting insurance as a business and may be assumed to have a level of knowledge significantly greater than that of the typical policyholder.

Nevertheless we ask if there is any reason not to apply our earlier proposals for business insurance to reinsurance.

SMALL BUSINESSES

As we explained earlier, our tentative view is that the residual duty of disclosure should be abolished in consumer cases but retained in business cases.

This leaves the question of whether small businesses should be treated as consumers or in the same way as larger businesses? Should a small and unsophisticated business be required to volunteer information to an insurer? Should a proportionate remedy apply in cases of negligent misrepresentation?

The Position of Small Businesses under the FOS Scheme

At present, the FOS makes a distinction between small businesses based on its assessment of the sophistication of the business in question. The most vulnerable businesses will be treated as consumers, while others will not. For example, in our survey a fish and chip shop was treated in the same way as a consumer, while an insurance broker was not. We found some cases where small businesses had been expected to volunteer information in the absence of questions. For example, the FOS held that a landlord should have revealed that his tenant was unsatisfactory even though the proposal form did not ask about this.

Options for Reform

In the joint Law Commissions' report on Unfair Contract Terms, we recommended that businesses with nine or fewer employees were often particularly vulnerable and required specific protection against unfair contract terms. We have considered whether micro businesses are also vulnerable in applying for insurance. Should they be treated as consumers and only required to answer the questions asked?

The problem with this approach is that some firms may have very few employees but be highly sophisticated. In the context of Unfair Contract Terms, we were told that in the capital markets it was common to use special purpose vehicles to conduct extremely complex deals. We developed several additional tests to exclude such companies, including a provision imposing a value limit on the contracts that could be reviewed and (on the grounds that they are already regulated) excluding all financial services contracts.

The same issues arise in insurance. A ship, for example, may be owned by a oneship company, and be managed using agents rather than employees. Obviously it may not be appropriate to say that an insurance contract affecting the vessel should not be subject to control because it is a financial services contract –that would beg the question of this review.

But otherwise similar exemptions may be needed. So in defining a small business, it would be necessary to look at the turnover and assets of the business, either instead of or as well as the number of employees. Any definition would also need to be based on factors that are transparent to an insurer. An insurer would need to know, for example, how the definition applied to an overseas entity that may be no more than a shell for a particular purpose.

There are two possible approaches. The first is to retain the duty of disclosure for small businesses, but only to the degree that would be reasonable in the circumstances (applying the test of materiality discussed earlier). We think this would enable the FOS to continue to take the approach it currently takes, by deciding that some small businesses are so similar to consumers that they should not be expected to volunteer information. It should also be possible for court to reach the same result, considering all the circumstances of the case.

The alternative would be to consider more sophisticated definitions of small businesses. We were particularly interested in the Norwegian approach, which disapplies the consumer regime when one of five criteria are satisfied:

(a) when the insurance relates to undertakings which at the time of concluding the contract, or at subsequent renewals, meet a minimum of two of the following requirements:

(1) the number of employees exceeds 250

(2) the sales earnings are a minimum of NOK 100 million according to the most recent annual accounts

(3) assets according to the most recent balance sheet are a minimum of NOK 50 million

(b) when the business takes place mostly abroad

(c) when the insurance relates to a ship under duty to register, cf. section 11 of the Maritime Act, or to installations as stated in section 33, subsection one, and sections 39 and 507 of the Maritime Act,

(d) when the insurance relates to aircraft, or

(e) when the insurance relates to goods in international transit, including transportation to and from the Norwegian Continental Shelf.

Using this sort of definition would ensure that foreign businesses and those taking out marine and aviation insurance would still be required to volunteer information. For domestic risks, the definition considers employees, turnover and assets. However, the test is complex, and brings back issues of how to define MAT, for example, that we had hoped to avoid.

We ask to what extent small businesses should be treated in the same way as consumers.

We ask how small businesses should be defined for this purpose.

8

INTRODUCTION SCOTTISH INSURANCE LAWS

BACKGROUND

The English and Scottish Law Commissions are conducting a joint review of insurance contract law. In January 2006 we published a Scoping Paper, explaining that the review would examine the law of misrepresentation, nondisclosure and breach of warranty in both consumer and commercial policies. We asked whether any other topics also needed to be considered. A feedback paper setting out the results of this consultation exercise is available on our website.

We intend to publish our first formal consultation paper in summer 2007, addressing misrepresentation, non-disclosure and breach of warranty. Before then, we are developing our ideas through a series of issues papers. The first paper considered misrepresentation and non-disclosure. This second paper deals with warranties and other similar contractual terms.

STATUS OF ISSUES PAPERS

This paper has been drafted by the teams working on the project at the English and Scottish Law Commissions. It has not been subject to formal scrutiny by Commissioners and does not represent fixed policy. It is simply intended to promote discussion before the formal consultation process begins, and should not be quoted as representing the views of either Commission.

OUR OBJECTIVES

Insurance works by pooling risks and resources. Our aim is to recommend reforms that strike a fair balance between the interests of insurers and insureds, so as to meet parties' legitimate expectations, without imposing unnecessary costs or restrictions.

Some of our proposals may result in more claims being paid, which would increase premiums. Where this corresponds to policyholders' legitimate expectations, consumers are probably willing to pay the small increase necessary to ensure that they are getting what they want. It does not make the insurance any less competitive. However, it is important that the impact should be considered. We will include an impact assessment in our final report. We have not included such an assessment in our issues papers, given that these papers merely indicate our provisional thoughts. Nevertheless, we would be interested in hearing views on the practical implications of the changes we are suggesting.

WHAT IS A WARRANTY?

The word "warranty" causes considerable confusion, as it is used in many different senses. In general contract law, a warranty is normally a term of minor importance, and a breach of warranty gives rise only to damages.1 Within the insurance industry, the word may be used to connote a variety of obligations placed on the insured. As a matter of insurance law, however, warranties are extremely important terms: the insured must comply with them strictly or face harsh consequences. Here we summarise the main characteristics of a warranty within insurance law, as set out in the Marine Insurance Act (MIA) 1906.

Undertakings for the Future and Affirmations of Fact

A wide variety of obligations on the insured can be given warranty status if the contract makes this sufficiently clear. Section 33(1) of the Marine Insurance Act (MIA) 1906 describes "promissory warranties" as terms by which the assured undertakes that some particular thing shall or shall not be done, or that some condition shall be fulfilled, or whereby he affirms or negatives the existence of a particular state of facts. In other words, warranties may apply to past or existing facts, or to future conduct.

Strict Compliance

The MIA states that a warranty "must be exactly complied with, whether it be material to the risk or not". So if an insured has "warranted" that certain facts are true, the warranty will be broken even if the answer made no difference, or if the insured was not at fault in any way. As we shall see, the insurer will be discharged from liability.

Later Remedy Irrelevant

Furthermore, once a breach has occurred, the fact that it has been remedied does not prevent the contract from being discharged. As section 34(2) states: Where a warranty is broken, the assured cannot avail himself of the defence that the breach has been remedied, and the warranty complied with, before loss.

For example, in *De Hahn v Hartley*, the insured warranted that the ship would sail from Liverpool with 50 hands. In fact, when the ship left Liverpool it had only 46 hands, though it picked up six more hands in Anglesey and had 52 hands at the time of the loss. The court held that the insurer's liability terminated when the ship left Liverpool. The insurer was not liable for any losses that arose after this date, however caused.

Automatic Discharge from Liability

Section 33(3) spells out that a warranty must be complied with exactly. If not, the insurer is discharged from liability under the contract, which means that an insurer is not liable for any claims arising after the breach. It states that if a warranty is not exactly complied with, then subject to any express provision in the policy, the insurer is discharged from liability as from the date of the breach of warranty, but without prejudice to any liability incurred by him before that date.

These words should be taken literally. In its 1980 report the Law Commission said that on a breach of warranty the insurer was "entitled to repudiate the policy". 4 In *The Good Luck*, Lord Goff criticised this formulation, saying that it was inappropriate to describe the insurer as "repudiating the policy".

It is more accurate to keep to "the carefully chosen words" of the 1906 Act and say that the insurer is discharged from liability as from the date of the breach. This means that, following breach, the insurer has a good defence to any claim without taking further action. The insurer may, however, waive the breach and restore their liability.

"Subject to Any Express Provision"

Section 33(3) is subject to any express terms of the policy. This means that the parties can contract out of automatic termination if they wish. For example, marine insurance contracts commonly include "held covered" clauses, which allow the policy to continue after the breach of warranty. Thus the Institute Time Clauses (Hull) include the following: Held covered in case of any breach of warranty as to cargo, trade, locality, towage, salvage services or date of sailing provided notice be given to the Underwriters immediately after receipt of advices and any amended term of cover and any additional premium required by them be agreed.

In other words, once the insured gives prompt notice of the breach, the insurer is obliged to provide additional cover, if necessary on amended terms and for an additional premium. Where the parties cannot agree on the terms or premium, the matter may be referred to a court or arbitration.

Creating a Warranty

Most warranties are created expressly by the parties. There is no single form of words that confers warranty status on a term. The use of the word "warranty" has been said to be indicative but by no means decisive.

As Lord Justice Rix put it in *HIH Casualty and General Insurance Ltd v New Hampshire Insurance Co*, It is a question of construction, and the presence or absence of the word "warranty" or "warranted" is not conclusive. One test is whether it is a term which goes to the root of the transaction; a second, whether it is descriptive or bears materially on the risk of loss; a third, whether damages would be an unsatisfactory or inadequate remedy.

The case concerned film finance insurance, in which the original insured had undertaken to make six films. This was held to be a warranty, even though the word warranty was not used, because it was a fundamental term with a direct bearing on the risk.

In marine insurance, the law will also imply certain warranties into the contract (which are set out in Appendix A).

A HIERARCHY OF TERMS

Warranties are best understood in the context of a hierarchy of different sorts of terms that impose obligations on policyholders. Warranties are the most severe, though breaches of other types of term may also extinguish insurers' liability for particular claims.

Within English law, It is possible to identify the following types of terms in insurance contracts:

(1) *Warranties* carry the most severe consequences for policyholders if they are breached. A breach discharges the insurer from any liability under the contract, even if the breach is minor or remedied later. In effect, compliance with a warranty is a condition precedent to liability arising under the policy as a whole.

(2) *Conditions precedent to a claim.* Here breach will discharge an insurer from liability to pay a particular claim, but will not affect other possible claims under the policies. Such conditions are most likely to be procedural, requiring (for example) notice of claims.

(3) Clauses which are "*descriptive of the risk*" for which the insurer is liable. These state that the insurer will only cover losses arising in particular circumstances, and if a loss arises in other circumstances, the insurer is not liable. Such terms are sometimes called "suspensive" conditions, on the basis that they merely suspend liability while a breach taking the risk outside the policy continues. If a policyholder remedies the problem the insurer resumes liability.

For example, in *Farr v Motor Traders Mutual Insurance* the policyholder insured two taxi-cabs, stating that they were only driven for one shift every 24 hours. For a short time, one of the cabs was driven for two shifts while the other was being repaired. The cab was then used for one shift a day in the normal way and a couple of months later was damaged in an accident. The Court of Appeal rejected the insurer's argument that the assured had breached a warranty. Instead the words were merely "descriptive of the risk". This meant that if the cab was driven for more than one shift per day, the risk would no longer be covered, but as soon as the owner resumed one-shift working, the insurer again became liable.

(4) *Innominate terms,* where the remedy for a breach depends on its seriousness. Where the breach is serious, the insurer may repudiate the policy (that is, treat the contract as terminated). Where it is minor, the remedy would be in damages only. In *Alfred McAlpine Plc v BAI (Run-Off),* it was suggested that a serious breach of a notification clause may lead to a rejection of the claim while a minor one may not.

(5) *Mere terms,* breach of which gives rise to a claim for damages, but which do not affect the insurer's liability to pay claims.

The category a term falls into is a matter of construction for the courts. There are many statements within the cases that any ambiguity should be resolved in favour of the insured. If the insurer wishes to treat a condition as a warranty or condition precedent, they must use clear words. They should not escape liability unless terms are put before policyholders "in words admitting of no possible doubt".

BASIS OF THE CONTRACT CLAUSES

The problems with warranties are exacerbated by the use of "basis of the contract" clauses. This is a device whereby potential policyholders are asked to sign a clause at the bottom of the proposal form, declaring that they warrant the accuracy of all the answers they have given.

The clause usually states that the answers "form the basis" of the contract. It is well established that such a clause may elevate the answers to contractual terms, even if the terms are not to be found in the policy itself.

The use of basis of the contract clauses means that an insurer may avoid liability for an inaccurate answer, even if the answer was not material, and even if it was given innocently.

For example, in *Dawson Ltd v Bonnin*, the insured was asked where a lorry was garaged. They inadvertently gave the firm's place of business in central Glasgow, though the lorry was usually kept on the outskirts. This did not increase the risk in any way (and arguably decreased it).

However, when the lorry was destroyed by fire, the insurers argued that the accuracy of the answer had been elevated to a warranty. Given the breach, the insurers were no longer liable. The House of Lords agreed (by a three to two majority) that even though the misrepresentation was immaterial, the insurers were not liable.

There has been widespread criticism of basis of the contract clauses. The 1980 report quoted judicial criticisms of such clauses dating from 1853. In 1908, Lord Justice Moulton said he wished he could "adequately warn the public against such practices". In 1927, Lord Wrenbury described their use as "mean and contemptible":

Here, upon purely technical grounds, [the insurers], having in point of fact not been deceived in any material particular, avail themselves of what seems to me the contemptible defence that although they have taken the premiums, they are protected from paying.

Despite these criticisms, however, the use of basis of the contract clauses has been upheld as recently as 1996. In *Unipac (Scotland) Ltd v Aegon Insurance* the company answered two questions on the proposal form inaccurately. They said they had been carrying on business for a year, while they had been incorporated for less than a year; and they said they were the sole occupiers of the premises, when they were not. Following a fire, the insurers refused to pay the claim.

The policyholders brought an action arguing that they had not warranted the accuracy of the answers, only that they were true to the best of their knowledge and belief. In the absence of a specific warranty, the insurer could avoid liability on the basis of a misrepresentation only if it was material. The Court of Session rejected these arguments, stating that the words used were clear. The court stressed the importance of freedom of contract in ringing terms:

We recognise that a consequence of holding that the declaration contains an express warranty of the truth of the answers to the questions in the proposal is that if there was an error in, for example, the postcode or telephone number of the proposer, the result would be that the defenders would be entitled to avoid the policy. That however is a consequence of the parties agreeing to an express warranty with the result that the defenders would have a right to avoid the policy if an answer was untrue whether or not the untrue item was material. We are not persuaded that that would be a ludicrous result. It is simply a consequence of what parties have agreed to by contract and parties are free to agree what they like.

While it is true that parties are free to agree what they like, normally they must do so in the contractual document itself. "Basis of the contract" clauses form an exception to this normal rule. Although in commercial policies the basis of the contract clause may often be referred to in the policy itself, this is not necessary under the current law. Clarke comments that it is difficult to square basis of the contract clauses "with the notion underlying the parole evidence rule", namely that a document such as a policy "which looks like the whole of the contract should be treated as the whole of the contract".

THE LAW COMMISSION

In 1980 the English Law Commission produced a report on non-disclosure and breach of warranty which recommended major reforms to prevent the unreasonable use of warranties to deny claims. In 2002, the British Insurance Law Association broadly endorsed the report's recommendations. The 1980 report is the starting point of our present project. Below we summarise the problems the 1980 report identified, and describe the recommendations that it made.

IDENTIFYING THE PROBLEMS

In 1980, the Law Commission set out four criticisms of the law of warranties and basis of the contract clauses:

(1) It seems quite wrong that the insurer should be entitled to demand strict compliance with a warranty which is not material to the risk and to repudiate the policy for a breach of it.

(2) Similarly it seems unjust that an insurer should be entitled to reject a claim for *any* breach of even a material warranty, no matter how irrelevant the breach may be to the loss.

(3) Warranties are of such importance that policyholders should be able to refer to a written document in which they are contained.

(4) Basis of the contract clauses are "a major mischief" because they enable insurers to repudiate policies for inaccurate statements even though:

(a) they are not material to the risk, or

(b) the policyholder could not be reasonably expected to know the true facts, or to have the means of knowing them.

THE RECOMMENDATIONS

The 1980 report attempted to cure these defects by both procedural and substantive means. First, the Law Commission recommended procedural safeguards affecting how warranties may be created. These would have effectively abolished basis of the contract clauses and required insurers to provide policyholders with written documents containing any warranties they had given. Substantively, policyholders would have a right to have their claim paid if they could show that a breach of warranty was unconnected with the risk. They could do this by showing that it was immaterial to the risk, or immaterial to the particular risk that had occurred, or could not have increased the risk that a loss would occur in the way it did occur.

Procedural Safeguards

Basis of the Contract Clauses should be Abolished

The recommendation on "basis of contract" clauses was designed to prevent statements of fact within the proposal form from being converted into warranties. Clause 9 of the draft Bill applied to "any statements affirming or denying the existence of, or giving his opinion with respect to, any fact or state of affairs at any time past or present". It provided that any such statement would not constitute a warranty if it were contained in a proposal form, or "made by reference to a provision in a proposal form";5 nor could it be converted into warranties by an incorporation clause within the contract itself.

The report states that the Commission did not "intend to ban specific undertakings by the insured as the existence of past or present facts".6 A specific fact could still constitute a warranty, provided it was in the policy itself. What insurers could not do was elevate the insured's answers into warranties *en bloc*. In other words, if a particular fact were so crucial to cover that the entire existence of the policy depended on it, the insurer must say so specifically in the policy. For example, a policy may state that the insured warranted that a building was made of brick and slate. However, a policy term could not convert all the answers the insured had given on a proposal form into warranties. The Commission wanted to prevent minor inaccuracies (such as a wrong address or telephone number) from invalidating cover. Nor could an answer be given warranty status by a notice on the proposal form. The term had to be in the contract itself.

Insurers should provide written statements as soon as practicable.

This recommendation was set out in clause 8(2) of the draft Bill. It states that an insurer shall not be entitled to rely on a breach of warranty unless the insured was supplied with "a written statement of the provision which constitutes the warranty". The statement must either be supplied at or before the time the contract was entered into, or "as soon thereafter as was practical in the circumstances of the case".

The report explained that if an insured has completed a proposal form and given answers relating to the future, the insurer could comply with this obligation by giving the insured a copy of the completed form. Normally, the insured would do this at or before the contract was entered into.

However, in some cases a warranty may be given and cover granted over the phone. Here the insurer should be required to confirm the warranty in writing as soon as practicable. This "may be done in a cover note, in a certificate of insurance, or even by letter".7

It is clearly right that any promissory warranty should be brought to the insured's attention as soon as possible. The problem with this provision, however, is that it could be complied with in a purely formalistic way. It does not ensure that the warranty is presented clearly or expressed in plain language. An insurer could comply with clause 8(2) even if they buried the warranty in a mass of small print.

Substantive Safeguards

The Working Paper Test

In its working paper the Law Commission had provisionally proposed a three-part test. For a term to be effective as a warranty, the insurer would have to show:

(1) that it was material to the risk, in the sense that it would influence a prudent insurer in deciding whether to accept the risk and if so at what premium; and

(2) the type of loss that occurred fell within the commercial purpose of the warranty. For example, the commercial purpose of a warranty that a vehicle should be kept roadworthy is intended to relate to the risks that arise when the car is being driven. A breach should not affect liability if the car is stolen.

Once the insurer had established this, it would on the face of it be entitled to reject the claim. However, the insurer would still be liable to pay if the *policyholder* could prove:

(3) that the breach could have had no possible connection with the actual loss that had occurred.

It was envisaged that this final test would place heavy onus on the policyholder. The working paper gave an example of a warranty in a fidelity policy that the insured employer would engage no one without first taking up satisfactory references.

The employer failed to take up references on employee A, who stole the employer's money. The paper argued that the insurer should "clearly be entitled to reject the claim, because the commercial purpose of the warranty was to guard against this very type of loss". Furthermore, "it should not be open to the insured to resist this by seeking to show, for instance, that A would have produced satisfactory or forged references if he had been asked for any". The court should not be invited to speculate on what might or might not have occurred. However, if the money were stolen by employee B, whose references were satisfactory, then the insured could show that there was no possible connection between the failure in relation to A and the actual loss. The test in the final report

Following consultation, the Law Commission changed its approach. It was persuaded that insurers should not have to show that a warranty was material to the risk. Instead it should be assumed to be material unless the insured showed that it would not have influenced a prudent underwriter. Similarly, it was decided that the onus should be on the insured to show that the type of loss did not fall within the commercial purpose of the warranty.

This led to a convoluted approach. If a claim were rejected for breach of warranty, the policyholder would have a choice between three possible lines of attack. The draft Bill would allow the insured to challenge the decision on any one of the following grounds:

(1) the warranty does not relate to a matter which is material.

(2) the warranty was intended to safeguard against a risk of a description "which does not include the event which gave rise to the claim"; or

(3) the breach of warranty could not have increased the risk that the event which gave rise to the claim would occur in the way in which it did in fact occur.

It is likely that in practice most policyholders would focus on (3), showing that the breach could not have increased the risk that the loss would occur in the way it did in fact occur.

Finally, the report recommended that insurers should be able to rely on a breach of warranty to repudiate policies in the future. To do this, they would need to serve a written notice on the insured. But the notice would not affect past claims.

The Law Commission argued that the issue of past claims and future repudiation should be treated separately. An insurer should be able to pay past claims and repudiate the policy for the future; it should also be entitled to reject claims, without repudiating in the future.

WHY JUST WARRANTIES? A PROBLEM WITH THE 1980 REPORT

There is a problem with the recommendations and draft bill in the 1980 report. The defence available to a policyholder only applies if the term is classified as a warranty. If a term is merely descriptive of the risk, the policyholder may no longer argue that the breach did not increase the loss. Yet policyholders' breach of such terms may also invalidate claims, even though there is no causal connection between the breach and the loss. Birds and Hird suggest that the fact the 1980 recommendations were limited to warranties in the strict sense was a major difficulty with the report. Its recommendations "might have been easily evaded by insurers resorting to the use" of other conditions and exceptions.

One example is where motor insurance is written on the basis that the vehicle will be used for one purpose and it is used for another purpose. A clause stating that a car is "insured only for private use" is usually construed as being "descriptive of the risk", following the *Farr* case. In other words, insurance cover is suspended when the car is being used for other purposes, but revives once the car is again used for private purposes. The consequences are not as severe as for breach of warranty, where a single episode of commercial use would discharge the insurer from all further liability. However, it is possible for a claim to be denied even though the policyholder could prove that the breach could not have increased the risk that the loss would occur in the way it did in fact occur.

This point was established in 1927 in *Roberts v Anglo-Saxon Insurance Ltd.* A car was said to be "warranted for commercial travelling", but suffered a fire while being used for another purpose. The arbitrator held that the insurer was nevertheless liable to pay the claim because the change of use did not in any way contribute to the fire or to the loss. Bankes LJ said this was a clear error of law:

> It is perfectly obvious that this is an error on the face of the award, because it is quite immaterial whether or not the fact that the car was being used in this way was or was not "a contributory cause of the fire or the actual cause or loss of the motor vehicle by the fire".

In *Murray v Scottish Automobile*, the car was insured for private use but was actually used as a taxi. It was damaged by fire while parked overnight in a garage. Again, the Court of Session held that the "private use" term was descriptive of the risk. Nevertheless, the insurer was not liable to pay the claim. Lord Sands stated that the time the car was parked in the garage "must be attributed to one use or the other". It was best seen as ancillary to the use to which the car has been put during the day. On this logic, the car was still being used as taxi when parked overnight, and the insurer was not liable to pay the claim.

This raises questions about how *Murray* would be decided if the 1980 report were to be implemented. If the term were to be construed as a warranty, then the policyholder could argue that the fire had nothing to do with the fact that the car had been used as a taxi during the day. If they succeeded, the insurer would be liable to meet the claim. However, if the term were merely descriptive of the risk, then the 1980 draft Bill would not apply. The insurer could successfully argue that the loss was outside the scope of the cover, as properly defined. This seems unduly formalistic. Whichever result is right, however, the same answer should apply to both warranties and descriptions of the risk. It should not depend on formalities about how the term has been written.

A more recent example is *Seddon v Binions*. Here a father was insured to drive for "social domestic and pleasure purposes". He occasionally helped his son out with the son's carpet laying business, although he did not get paid for it. One Sunday, the father, son and the son's employee were laying a carpet, when the son's employee suffered a toothache.

The father drove the employee to the dentist in his son's car and suffered a serious accident. The Court of Appeal held that the essential character of that journey was that the father was using the son's car for a business purpose. The father's insurance did not apply to the journey that had taken place, and the insurers were not liable to meet the claim.

In *Seddon*, the dispute was between two insurers. The son's car was insured with a different company, who met the cost of the accident. If the policyholder had stood to suffer a large loss, the Court might have interpreted the facts in a more sympathetic light. However, the essential problem remains. Even a very minor and technical breach may take a loss outside the description of the risk. It cannot be right to apply one set of protections to warranties and a lesser set to exceptions.

The issue is not simply confined to use clauses. There are many other examples. It is common for motor insurance policies to state that a vehicle should not be driven in an unroadworthy condition. This may be written as descriptive of the risk, to say the insurer is not liable while the vehicle is being driven in an unroadworthy condition. Alternatively, it may be written as a warranty, that "the insured shall take all reasonable steps to maintain the vehicle in a roadworthy condition".

There are cases where a car is in an unroadworthy condition, but the defect does not cause an accident. In *Conn v Westminster Motor Insurance*, for example, a taxi was driven with worn tyres, but Lord Justice Salmon commented, If one thing is plain in this case it is that whatever did cause this accident, it had nothing to do with the dangerous and inefficient condition of the tyres.

However, the insurer still escaped liability. In *Conn* it did not matter if the term was a warranty or an exception. As the defect was current at the time of the accident, the insurer was not liable. It would not make any sense to permit an insured to argue lack of causal connection in the case of warranties, but not in the case of exceptions.

That said, if one extended the protections in the 1980 report to all exceptions that define the risk, the impact on the insurance industry could be considerable. Take for example, a standard exception in a fire policy, that the property is not covered if it is left unoccupied for more than

30 days. The risk of vandalism or arson is clearly increased if a property is left unoccupied; and there is a greater risk that a fire might spread. But many fires will not be related to the fact the property is unoccupied: suppose, at an extreme, that the fire is caused by an aeroplane crashing onto the premises.

The fact that the line between warranties and descriptions of the risk is so narrow has several implications for this area of law. On the one hand, it allows the courts to avoid the harsh effects of warranties by reclassifying terms as descriptions of the risk.

On the other hand, it would allow insurers to escape the effect of any reforms that were limited only to warranties. The Unfair Terms in Consumer Contract Regulations may offer a partial solution, in that they permit a court to find that an unclear and unfair exclusion has no effect. However, they only apply to consumer insurance. Furthermore there is some uncertainty about the way the regulations apply to descriptions of the risk in insurance contracts.

ARE WARRANTIES STILL A PROBLEM?

Alternative Methods of Protection

One argument against reform is that warranties are no longer a problem in practice. It has been suggested that any potential difficulties with the law can be dealt with by the courts as a matter of construction.

As far as consumers are concerned, three further types of protection are available:

(1) voluntary statements of practice and Financial Services Authority (FSA) rules;

(2) an assessment of fairness under the Unfair Terms in Consumer Contracts Regulations 1999; and

(3) the Financial Ombudsman Service (FOS).

Below we outline the protections provided by each of these approaches, and consider how far they remove or change the need to reform the law of warranties.

THE CONSTRUCTION APPROACH

It is well-established that warranties should be construed strictly, against the party who has put them forward (in practice, usually the insurer). This common law rule is now supplemented in consumer insurance by the Unfair Terms in Consumer Contracts Regulations, which state that "if there is a doubt about the meaning of a written term, the interpretation which is most favourable to the consumer shall prevail".

The normal remedy against an insurer's unreasonable use of a warranty is for the court to hold that the term is not truly a warranty, but something else (such as a clause descriptive of the risk) or that the term does not cover the issue in hand. Over the years, the courts have found several ways to attack the unreasonable use of warranties and these methods are used extensively in commercial cases.

(1) The warranty applies only to past or present facts, and not to the future. For example, in *Hussain v Brown*, the insured had signed a proposal form to say that their premises were fitted with an intruder alarm.5 This was said to be the basis of the contract. The statement was true at the time of the contract, though the firm later failed to pay the charges and the alarm service was suspended. The Court of Appeal held that the statement on the proposal form related only to present facts and did not make any promises about the future. Any continuing warranty would be a "draconian term" and "if underwriters want such protection then it is up to them to stipulate for it in clear terms".

(2) The warranty is relevant to only some sections of the policy. For example, in *Printpak v AGF Insurance Ltd*, the insured had taken out a "commercial inclusive" policy, which covered a range of risks, including fire and theft. The theft section included a warranty that the insured would maintain a burglar alarm. Meanwhile Condition stated that a failure to comply with any warranty would invalidate any claim. The insured suffered a fire while the alarm was not working. The Court of Appeal held that the policy was not a seamless document, but instead consisted of separate schedules, each concerned with a different type of risk. Despite the wording of Condition, the alarm warranty only applied to the theft risk and not the fire risk.

(3) The clause is not a true warranty but merely descriptive of the risk. As we have seen, in *Farr v Motor Traders Mutual Insurance*, the Court of Appeal rejected the insurer's argument that a statement that taxis were to be driven for only one shift a day was a warranty. Instead, the statement described the risk. Cover was suspended while the taxi was used for two shifts a day; and once the owner resumed one shift the insurer became liable again.

(4) The wording of the warranty does not apply to the facts in question. The leading case is *Provincial Insurance Co v Morgan*. Here coal merchants declared that their lorry would be used for coal, which became the basis of the contract. On the day of the accident, the lorry was also used to carry Forestry Commission timber. However, at the time, the timber had been unloaded and only coal was on-board. The House of Lords held an endorsement on the policy stating that the use was "transportation of own goods in connection with the insured's own business" did not

mean that the vehicle was to be used *exclusively* for the insured's own goods. On "a strict but reasonable construction" the declaration and the clause only meant that transporting coal was to be the normal use. Transporting other goods would not terminate liability under the policy.

How far can construction be used to remove unfairness? *Kler Knitwear*

A difficult question is whether the courts should be prepared to disregard the clear language of the policy in order to achieve justice between the parties. *Kler Knitwear v Lombard General Insurance Co* is an example of a case where the judge arguably went beyond merely resolving ambiguity in order to protect the policyholder from an unfair outcome.12 Here the policyholders had agreed that their sprinkler system would be inspected 30 days after renewal. In fact, the inspection was about 60 days late and showed that the system was working. The factory later suffered storm damage (which was wholly unconnected with the sprinklers). Mr Justice Morland accepted in principle that if on a proper construction of the clause, the parties intended it to be a warranty then the Court "must uphold that intention" however harsh and unfair the consequences. However, this particular clause was merely "a suspensive condition", limiting the risk.

The surprising thing about *Kler Knitwear* was that the term was clearly stated to be a warranty and the policy later went on to spell out the consequences, namely that non-compliance would bar any claim, "whether it increases the risk or not".

Birds and Hird comment that,

It is difficult to see how the insurer could have stipulated this in any clearer terms. The term itself was called a warranty and was drafted in clear and intelligible language and the consequences of noncompliance were spelled out. In *Kler Knitwear,* the judge would appear to be going further than merely resolving an ambiguity in contractual drafting in favour of the ɒsured. Instead he is replacing a consequence that "would be utterly absurd and make no business sense"14 with one that is fairer to the insured.

Cases such as *Kler Knitwear* provide a partial solution to the problem of warranties. We have been told that the courts' approach to construction discourages insurers from taking purely technical points or attempting to use warranties in a wholly unreasonable way. However, it does so at the cost of introducing uncertainty and confusion into the law. As each clause must be interpreted on its own wording, it encourages similar issues to be litigated repeatedly. And in some cases, the reasoning required to produce a fair result is convoluted to the point of incomprehensibility.

The problem of notification clauses: the rise and fall of innominate terms.

The difficulties associated with "the construction approach" can be illustrated by looking at the way the English courts have approached a different sort of term – namely notification clauses. These have caused particular problems in insurance contracts. In some cases it may be wholly reasonable to make prompt notification a condition precedent to the insurers' liability. In other cases, it may be disproportionate to deprive the policyholder of their entire claim simply because of a minor delay that caused the insurer no real prejudice.

In *Alfred McAlpine Plc v BAI (Run-Off),* Lord Justice Waller attempted to deal with this problem by developing the concept of "innominate terms". He applied the principles set out in the *Hongkong Fir* case,*17* to say for some terms the consequences of a breach may depend on its seriousness.

Some breaches may be so serious that they would entitle the insurer to repudiate the claim, while "minor failures" would result in damages only.18 In the *BAI* case, the insurer remained liable to pay the claim as it had not been prejudiced by a late notification, which amounted to only a minor breach of the condition. However, if the insurer has suffered real prejudice because, for example, it has been prevented from preparing a defence to a liability claim, then it would cease to be liable to pay the claim.

The "innominate term" classification was welcomed as providing greater flexibility in the remedies available. However, a recent Court of Appeal judgment, *Friends Provident Life and Pensions v Sirius International Insurance*, has cast doubt on the reasoning in the BAI case.

In *Friends Provident*, the insured had failed to notify the excess layer underwriters that a potential claim for pensions mis-selling may exceed the amount insured under the primary layer. This was a breach of Clause of the policy. Clause was not worded as a condition precedent; nor did it suggest that a breach would absolve the insurers from liability for the claim. However, the insurers argued that it was an "innominate term". The breach should be regarded as sufficiently serious to absolve the insurers from liability to meet the claim.

Lord Justice Mance disagreed. He pointed out that breach of an innominate term would only entitle an insurer to repudiate the contract as a whole; it would not entitle an insurer to merely reject one specific claim. And it "was not easy to conceive" that a breach of an ancillary term could be fundamental to the contract as a whole. The argument that a serious breach of a notice clause would discharge an insurer from liability to pay that particular claim would introduce a new doctrine of "partial repudiatory breach". No such doctrine existed and there was no reason to introduce it.

Lord Justice Mance argued that if the insurers had intended Clause to operate as a condition precedent to liability for a particular claim, they should have worded it in those terms. As they had not done so, their remedy lay in damages only. Where insurers failed to draft notification clauses as conditions precedent, they did not require additional protection:

English law is strict enough as it is in insurers' favour. I see no reason to make it stricter.

Sir William Aldous agreed, though Lord Justice Waller Dissented.

It is true that if insurers do not draft clauses as conditions precedent to liability, then the decision that their remedy lies in damages only favours policyholders. The problem, however, is that the *Friends Provident* decision will encourage insurers to draft every ancillary provision as a condition precedent. And if the term is clearly a condition precedent, the courts will be required to interpret it as such, however minor and unimportant the breach. This could import an untoward element of technicality and rigidity into the law, whereby claims are denied for minor breaches by policyholders that cause no real prejudice to insurers.

Although the case law on notification clauses is not directly applicable to warranties, these cases illustrate some of the weaknesses of the construction approach. First, the law is uncertain, and is likely to cause further litigation. Secondly, each case depends on the particular words used. Insurers are likely to respond to unfavourable decisions by attempting to achieve the desired effect with different words.

The Construction Approach: Conclusion

Courts' willingness to construe warranties against the interests of insurers provides a partial solution to the unfairness inherent in the existing law. It does so at the cost of adding complexity and uncertainty to the law. We anticipate repeated litigation over both warranties and notification clauses.

Furthermore, there are still harsh decisions that cause injustice to policyholders. In *Unipac (Scotland) Ltd v Aegon Insurance*, for example, the Court of Session upheld a basis of the contract clause which converted all the statements in the proposal form into warranties.22 We do not think that courts' willingness to construe clauses against the interests of insurers removes the need for reform.

THE ABI STATEMENTS OF PRACTICE AND FSA RULES

Insurance companies have long argued that the defects in the present law can be remedied through voluntary action. In 1977 the Association of British Insurers agreed to two statements of practice: one for general insurance and one for life. The 1980 report explained that the statements were the result of concern about the decision to exclude insurance from the Unfair Contract Terms Act 1977, and were designed to reassure consumers that they would not be dealt with unfairly. The statements covered both warranties and "basis of the contract" clauses. Below we look at each issue in turn. We then consider the FSA's more general initiative to encourage insurers to treat their customers fairly.

Provisions on Warranties

Statements of Practice

The 1977 Statement of General Insurance Practice (SGIP) dealt with the perceived problems with warranties by stating that: Except where fraud, deception or negligence is involved, an insurer will not unreasonably repudiate liability to indemnify a policyholder... on grounds of a breach of warranty or condition, where the circumstances of the loss are unconnected with the breach. The references to deception or negligence were later removed, so as to confine the right to repudiate only where fraud is involved. The 1986 version of SGIP read: An insurer will not repudiate liability to indemnify a policyholder on the grounds of a breach of warranty or condition where the circumstances of the loss are unconnected with the breach unless fraud is involved.

The 1977 Statement of Long-Term Insurance Practice (SLIP) did not specifically refer to warranties at all, and merely said that "an insurer would not unreasonably reject a claim". However, in 1986 SLIP was revised, to be similar to SGIP.

In 1980 we made three criticisms of the 1977 Statements:

(1) The statements only covered private (that is, consumer) insurance, while the problems covered both consumers and businesses.

(2) The provision in effect conferred "a discretion on insurers to repudiate a policy on technical grounds if they suspect fraud but are unable to prove it".

(3) The statements lacked the force of law "so that an insured would have no legal remedy if an insurer fails to act in accordance with them".

We concluded that far from being an argument against reform, the statements were "evidence that the law is unsatisfactory and needs to be changed".

FSA Rules

The Statement of General Insurance Practice has now been abolished and replaced by ICOB 7.3.6. For long-term insurance, SLIP has been supplemented by COB 8A.2.6. ICOB Rule 7.3.6 states that insurers may not: except where there is evidence of fraud, refuse to meet a claim made by a retail customer on the grounds: (c) in the case of a general insurance contract, of breach of warranty or condition, unless the circumstances of the claim are connected with the breach.

COB 8A.2.6 is in similar terms, except that it only applies to breaches of warranty and not conditions. It goes on to state that the warranty must be "material to the risk" and must be "drawn to the attention of the policyholder before the conclusion of the contract".

These provisions replicate the difficulties identified with the 1977 Statement. First they only cover retail (that is, consumer) insurance. Secondly, they continue to permit insurers to repudiate claims where they suspect but cannot prove fraud: although the insurer must show some evidence of fraud it does not have to be conclusive evidence.

Thirdly, the rules fail to give an insured a normal legal remedy if the insurer does not act in accordance with the rules. It is true that in the case of widespread breach, the FSA may bring disciplinary action against the insurer, leading to fines or (ultimately) withdrawal of authorisation. However, the issue is more likely to arise in the context of an individual claim. Individuals may have a remedy under section 150(1) of the Financial Services and Markets 2000, which states that A contravention by an authorised person of a rule is actionable at the suit of a private person who suffers loss as a result of the contravention, subject to the defences and other incidents applying to actions for breach of statutory duty.

This would suggest that if the matter were to be raised before a court, the court would have to find for the insurer on the basis of the strict law. Then (in the same or separate proceedings) the consumer could claim damages on the ground that the point should not have been taken.

This is a solution of a kind but we wonder whether in practice any consumer would claim damages for breach of statutory duty because of the costs involved. In addition, the result is that the law is at best hard to understand and arguably is incoherent. The COB and ICOB rules are difficult to reconcile with the decision in *The Good Luck,* that following a breach of warranty, the insurer need not take steps to repudiate a policy but is instead automatically discharged from liability.

It would appear that an insurer may breach an FSA rule by doing no more than refusing to meet a claim for which they are not liable. This overlap of law and regulation is neither clear nor simple, and has the potential to bring the law into disrepute. We do not think that FSA rules remove the need for reform. Rather, like the statements, they appear to be evidence that the law is unsatisfactory and needs to be changed.

Provisions on "Basis of the Contract" Clauses

This issue was not directly addressed in the 1977 statement. However, the 1986 SGIP effectively outlawed their use. Clause 1(b) said: Neither the proposal form nor the policy shall contain any provision converting the statement as to past or present fact in the proposal form into warranties. But insurers may require specific warranties about matters which are material to the risk.

In other words, insurers agreed that they would no longer put provisions on proposal forms that automatically converted the answers given into warranties. If they wished to include warranties in the contract, they would have to be specific and material to the risk.

The Long-Term Statement, however, took a less robust approach. It made an exception where the policyholder took out a policy on the life of someone else (so called "life of another" policies). Here insurers could ask general questions about the life to be assured and convert them en masse into warranties. However, insurers undertook not to reject a claim on the basis of a misrepresentation unless the statement was both material and within the knowledge of the proposer. As the law allows insurers to avoid policies for material misrepresentations in any event, it is not clear exactly what life insurers gain by turning proposal form answers into warranties in these circumstances. Presumably, it removes the need to show that a particular statement induced them to enter into the contract: it would be enough that the statement would be material to a prudent underwriter.

In 2004, when SGIP was replaced by ICOB, the prohibition on basis of the contract clauses was removed. Rule 7 does not include any provisions relating to basis of the contract clauses. We have not been able to find any justification for this change at the time it was made. However, the ABI has since told us that they believe that use of such clauses would be prevented by the general principle that insurers should treat their customers fairly. They therefore believe that specific provisions are unnecessary.

Treating Customers Fairly

The FSA publishes 11 high level "Principles for Business", to be found in the PRIN sourcebook. They are part of a move away from prescriptive rules to principles-based regulation. Principle 6 states that: A firm must pay due regard to the interests of its customers and treat them fairly.

As part of an FSA initiative, insurers are required to demonstrate that they are building the principle of treating customers fairly into all that they do.

In July 2006, the FSA published the General Insurance Cluster report, highlighting examples of good and bad practice in this area. One example given of poor practice was that: Some insurers refuse claims for unconnected breaches (eg not paying out on a claim related to an escape of water due to an alarm breach).

The FSA was particularly keen to improve the quality of information insurers give customers. They point out that although firms are required to make significant and unusual exclusions clear to their customers, they do not always do so, "but at times overwhelm them with information so they are unable to pick out the key messages". However, there are many examples of good practice in this area, where for example, home insurers make it clear "exactly what is expected of customers under a policy if they have a burglar alarm or other home security device".

UNFAIR TERMS IN CONSUMER CONTRACTS

A major change since the 1980 report is that unfair terms in consumer insurance may now be subject to review. Although insurance contracts generally are not subject to the Unfair Contract Terms Act 1977, consumer insurance is covered by the EU Directive on Unfair Terms in Consumer Contracts, and the implementing Unfair Terms in Consumer Contract Regulations. Unfortunately the impact of the Regulations on insurance contracts, and in particular on warranties, is complex. A detailed explanation is needed.

Which terms may be reviewed?

The Directive allows a court to review the fairness of all non-negotiated terms in a consumer contract, except for core terms. These are defined in Article 4(2): Assessment of the unfair nature of the terms shall relate neither to the definition of the main subject matter of the contract nor to the adequacy of the price and remuneration, on the one hand, as against the services or goods supplied in exchange, on the other, in so far as these terms are in plain intelligible language.

This somewhat cumbersome sentence is re-written in Regulation 6(2): In so far as it is in plain intelligible language, the assessment of fairness of a term shall not relate to

(a) the definition of the main subject matter of the contract, or

(b) to the adequacy of the price or remuneration, as against the goods or services supplied in exchange.

In *Director General of Fair Trading v First National Bank Plc*, the House of Lords explained that the core terms provisions should be interpreted narrowly.

As Lord Bingham put it, the object of the Regulations and Directive "would plainly be frustrated" if the definition of core terms were "so broadly interpreted as to cover any terms other than those falling squarely within it". Lord Steyn confirmed that the provision must be given a restrictive interpretation, or "the main purpose of the scheme would be frustrated by endless formalistic arguments about whether a provision is a definitional or an exclusionary provision".

There has been some debate about how far these provisions apply to insurance contracts. The insurance industry has long opposed the idea that such terms should be subject to judicial review, and was very concerned at the possible impact of the Directive. To assuage their fears, the Directive included the following words in Recital 19: For the purposes of this Directive, assessment of unfair character shall not be made of terms which describe the main subject matter of the contract nor the quality/price ratio of the goods or services supplied.... It follows, inter alia, that in insurance contracts, the terms which clearly define or circumscribe the insured risk and the insurer's liability shall not be subject to such assessment since these restrictions are taken into account in calculating the premium paid by the consumer.

This has been taken to mean that any terms which "clearly define or circumscribe the insured risk" are core terms within the meaning of the Directive and Regulations, and therefore exempt from review. We examine this argument in more detail below. To make the discussion easier to follow, we deal first with exceptions and then with warranties.

Exceptions and UTCCR

Are Exceptions "Price" Terms?

The words in Recital 19 do not mean that an exception within an insurance contract "relates to the adequacy of the price". An insurer may well take such exceptions into account in calculating the price, but this could be true of any term within the contract. As Lord Steyn put it in *First National Bank*: After all, in a broad sense all terms of the contract are in some way related to the price or remuneration. That is not what is intended.

First National Bank itself was about the terms of a loan. Clearly, the interest rate itself was the price (and not subject to review) but a clause stating that the same rate was payable on default was merely incidental to the substance of the bargain. The House of Lords held it was subject to review. A price escalation clause would also be subject to review "or there would be a gaping whole in the system"41 (even if, presumably, the supplier had taken account of the presence of such escalation clause in calculating the initial price).

Do exceptions "define the main subject matter of the contract"?

Although an exception to the cover is not a price term, there is a strong argument that it does define the main subject matter of the contract. Clearly, the main subject matter of an insurance contract is the cover the policyholder receives. MacGillivray considers that the exemption extends to terms which describe the perils insured against and specify the measure of indemnity afforded by the cover, but not to procedural requirements to give notice of claims. Birds and Hird also argue that the definition of the main subject matter should be taken to include both "the risks covered and excepted". They point out that the Regulations must be read subject to Recital 19, which refers to terms which "clearly define or circumscribe the insurer's liability".

This was the view taken by Mr Justice Buckley in *Bankers Insurance Co v South*. A holiday-maker had taken out a travel insurance policy which exempted "compensation or other costs arising from accidents involving ... possession of any ... motorised waterborne craft". Whilst riding a jet ski he had been involved in an accident which seriously injured another jet skier. The victim then attempted to argue, first, that the exemption did not apply to jet skis. Secondly, if it did, it was an unfair term within the meaning of the regulations. Buckley J held that the term was in plain intelligible language and therefore exempt from scrutiny. Unfortunately for our purposes, he did not develop this point. The judge also said that in any event he could see nothing unfair in the term. It was available to the holiday-maker, and he could have read it if he had wished. He also pointed out that the insurance was relatively cheap.

We accept that an exception to cover may be taken as defining the cover: for example, a clause that states cover is limited to roadworthy vehicles has the potential to be a core term. However, it does not follow that all exceptions are exempt from review as being core terms. There are two restrictions. First, the definition of the main subject matter of the contract is only exempt from review "so far as it is in plain intelligible language". Secondly, a term cannot be "the definition of the main subject matter of the contract" if it is substantially different to what the consumer reasonably expected. We take these points in turn in the paragraphs that follow. Does an exception have to be in plain language?

The exclusion from review only applies to core terms "in so far as these terms are in plain intelligible language". If an exclusion is not clearly worded, it will not be treated as a core term, and will be subject to review for fairness. As MacGillivray states, "failure to word a core term of the insurance clearly will result in it losing its exemption from assessment for fairness".

This requirement of the Directive is not universally accepted. Clarke, for example, includes a footnote in which he refers to the argument that "if core terms are not plain and intelligible they shall be assessed for fairness". He describes this result as "startling", "new" and having "no basis in the Directive". He refers to the opening words in Recital 19, that "assessment of unfair character shall not be made of terms which describe the main subject matter of the contract".

He points out that this opening phrase is "unqualified", and does not state that the term must be in plain intelligible language. We do not think this view is correct. Recital 19 must be subject to the clear words of Article 4(2), which states that the exemption from assessment only applies "in so far as these terms are in plain intelligible language". Furthermore Recital 19 itself is confined to terms which "*clearly* define or circumscribe the insured risk". Exceptions that are substantially different from what the consumer reasonably expects.

Recital 20 suggests that the requirement is not just one of plain language. It says that contracts should not only be drafted in plain, intelligible language but also that "the consumer should actually be given an opportunity to examine all the terms".

This leads to the question of whether a term that is itself clearly worded can be exempt from review as a core term if it is not what the consumer reasonably expected, for instance if it is hidden among the small print of a contract where consumers are extremely unlikely to read it. When the two Law Commissions examined the law on unfair terms in contracts, we endorsed the view put forward by the Office of Fair Trading that a term only defines the main subject matter of the contract if it is part of the way consumers perceived the bargain. As the OFT put it: A supplier would surely find it hard to sustain the argument that a contract's main subject matter was defined by a term which a consumer had been given no real opportunity to see and read before signing.

We explained that: In a contract for a "holiday with travel by air", a clause in the "small print" allowing the company, in the event of air traffic control strikes, to carry the consumer by rail and sea seems to be reviewable for fairness; but it can be argued that if the holiday is "with travel by air or, in the event of strikes, by rail and sea", the option of mode of travel *might* be part of the definition of the main subject matter.

In other words, whether the term relates to the definition of the subject matter depends (at least in part) on how the deal is presented to the consumer.

Applying the same principle to an insurance contract, take a case where a policy was sold as "insurance for winter sports adventure holidays", but one of the lengthy policy terms excluded off-piste skiing, and no particular attempt was made to bring this to the proposer's attention. The exclusion of off-piste skiing would not be a core term. However, if the policy were sold as "suitable for skiing on piste", the same term might be exempt from review, provided it was presented in a plain intelligible way.

Our draft Bill on Unfair Contract Terms sought to clarify the law in this area, without changing it. Under clause 4(2), a term is excluded from review if it defines the main subject matter of the contract provided the definition is-

(a) transparent and

(b) substantially the same as the definition the consumer reasonably expected.

The draft Bill goes on to define "transparent" as meaning:

(a) expressed in reasonably plain language,

(b) legible,

(c) presented clearly, and

(d) readily available to any person likely to be affected by the contract term or notice in question.

In other words, a clause that excluded fire cover if the house was unoccupied might be exempted from review, but only if it were what a consumer would reasonably expect, and if it were readily available, presented clearly, legible and expressed in reasonably plain language. If the clause were merely one of the small print terms, and no special steps had been taken to bring it to the consumer's attention, it would no longer be a core term, and a court could review it to see if it was fair.

It is not necessarily sufficient for the term to be in plain language. An exception or other clause defining the risk may be in plain language without necessarily being clearly presented, or even readily available. The Directive requires that the term relates to the main subject matter of the contract. It would be difficult to argue that an exception or definition of which consumers were quite reasonably unaware defined the main subject matter of the contract. Such a term would therefore be subject to review for fairness. It does not follow that a court will necessarily treat it as unfair, but if it is substantially different from what the consumer reasonably expected and it is not readily accessible, there must be a risk that the court will hold it to be an unfair term.

We would add that in practice it is probably necessary to include the exception in the documentation (the proposal form or descriptive summary of the policy) that the consumer is given before the contract is made. Merely to include it in the policy document will not suffice, even if the proposal form or summary refers to the policy document. Consumers' reasonable expectations will not be set by terms they only discovered after entering into the contract. Even if the consumer received the terms in advance, a term is unlikely to define the main subject matter of the contract unless it was highlighted in some way.

The Effect on Warranties

Here we consider what effect the Unfair Terms in Consumer Contract Regulations have on warranties in consumer insurance contracts. The two limitations that may prevent an exception being a core term apply equally to a warranty. In the case of warranties, however, there are additional complications.

Take the example where the consumer warranted that they would fit a particular type of mortice lock. The question is whether the term is subject to review, or whether it is exempt because it "defines the main subject matter of the contract".

Just like an exception, the warranty would need to be in plain intelligible language. Equally, applying the reasoning we adopted in our project on Unfair Terms in Contracts, we think warranties, just like exceptions, would have to be part of the way the deal was presented to the consumer. The key terms document would need to make it plain that coverage was dependent on the lock being in place. However, with warranties there are possible restrictions that do not apply to exceptions.

Do warranties define the subject-matter of the contract?

First, we have wondered whether a warranty, however clearly worded and prominently set out, can ever be a "core term", simply because it does not describe the subject-matter of the contract. In effect it circumscribes the insurer's liability if the right lock is not installed, and might be thought of as the kind of "incidental" or "subsidiary" term that the House of Lords, in its decision in *DGFT v First National Bank plc*, recognised as not being "core". On reflection, however, we do not think this argument is correct. A warranty is correctly interpreted as an obligation on the insured, and there is no reason why (if it is clear and "reasonably expected") it should not be as "core" as the obligation to pay the premium.

The Effect of Warranties and Reasonable Expectations

A second restriction does seem to bite on warranties. We think that unless the insurer expressly spells out in full the effect of a breach of the warranty, it will be subject to review because it will almost inevitably fail the "reasonable expectations" test.

Consider the legal effect of a breach of the warranty. It will discharge the insurer from liability under policy automatically, so that there is no liability for any loss even if the matter warranted was immaterial, or the loss was completely unrelated to the breach (for example, flood damage). The insurer is discharged from liability even if the breach of warranty has been cured before the claim arose. As we argued earlier, it is most unlikely that these results accord with the reasonable expectations of any insured, least of all a consumer-unless he or she happens to be an insurance lawyer. Thus for the warranty to be exempt as a "core term", the consequences of a breach of a warranty would have to be spelled out in full, in clear and intelligible language and in a way that left the consumer in no doubt what to expect.

If the term were not sufficiently central to the way the bargain was presented to be a core term, the court would need to consider whether it was fair. It should be noted that under the UTCCR, the court is required to assess the fairness of the term at the time the contract was made. It is not asked to assess whether the term has been applied fairly in the particular circumstances of the loss. Thus if the term gives the insurer the right to avoid even when the breach of warranty was immaterial, it will be no answer that in the particular facts the loss that has been incurred was caused directly by the breach of warranty. If the warranty as a whole was unfair, the insurer simply cannot rely on it at all.

It might be argued that most warranties are fair on their face. The unfairness arises only because of the way they are applied. However, before assessing the fairness of a term the court must interpret it. Suppose, for example, that an insurer seeks to rely on the lock warranty to reject a claim for flood damage.

The court would first have to decide whether the term was a true warranty, and was intended to exclude flood claims in this way. If the court accepts the insurer's case that the term has a wide meaning, then it is likely to hold that the term is unfair. The court may be influenced by the fact that this use of the term specifically breaches ICOB Rule 7.3.6. As a result, the term would not be binding on the consumer, and the insurer could not rely on it to avoid paying the claim. If the court gives the term a narrow meaning, to merely except burglary claims while the lock is not fitted, then the term is more likely to be considered fair – but it would not assist the insurer to resist liability for flood damage.

Preventive Powers

A major innovation in the 1994 Regulations was that enforcement was not left to the parties alone. Instead, the Director General of Fair Trading was empowered to bring proceedings for an injunction (or interdict) against suppliers using unfair terms in their contracts with consumers.

In 1999, the list of enforcement organisations was extended, and in 2001 the Financial Services Authority was added. The FSA is now the organisation primarily responsible for preventing insurers from including unfair terms within their contracts.

The FSA has reached agreements with insurance companies to alter terms: for example, the FSA complained about a cash-back scheme underwritten by insurers, which only met claims if consumers submitted numerous forms within strict time limits.

The insurers agreed that they would accept claims within 6 months of the specified dates and would issue replacement documents on request.

In July 2006 the FSA took action against a term in a legal expenses insurance policy which bore some similarities to a warranty. It stated that "cover will end at once" if the insured dismissed their appointed representative, or if the representative refused to act for the insured.

This was thought to be unfair as the insured may have a legitimate reason for dismissing the representative (for example, in the event of fraud), or the legal representative may refuse to act for the consumer for reasons beyond the consumer's control. Following FSA intervention, the insurer rewrote the term to state that the cover will only end if the insured dismisses the representative without good reason, or the representative refuses to act for a good reason.

The Impact of the Unfair Terms in Consumer Contracts Regulations

The regulations have been in place since 1994, applying to all contracts entered into after 1 July 1995. So far, they appear to have had surprisingly little impact on the insurance industry. With the exception of the *Bankers* case, we have not located any cases in which the issue was argued in the courts.

The Regulations have the potential to provide protection to consumers. However, we do not think that in practice they give consumers adequate protection. Here, we have attempted to spell out how the Regulations affect the case of a warranty applied to a non-causally connected loss, but it has not been an easy task: it has produced considerable discussion among members of the team and with our advisers.

Any consumer attempting to argue such a case before the courts would need to overcome several hurdles: first, that the warranty was not a core term or, if it was, it was not in plain language; and secondly that it was unfair at the time the contract was entered into. We think that even in consumer cases it would be useful to spell out that a breach of warranty should not absolve the insurer from liability to pay an unrelated claim. This test looks not at the fairness of the term at the time of the contract, but at the way it is applied to the particular circumstances of the claim.

THE FINANCIAL OMBUDSMAN SERVICE

The Financial Ombudsman Service (FOS) has a general discretion to decide cases according to what is fair and reasonable. In practice, dissatisfied consumers are more likely to take a case to the FOS than to court.

To understand how the FOS currently approaches disputes over policy terms, we read 50 final ombudsman decisions concerning terms in consumer policies. We are very grateful to FOS for allowing us access to these cases.

Issues of Causal Connection

Our brief analysis of ombudsman cases suggests that warranties are not common in consumer cases. Although a few exclusions appeared to be written in wide terms, it is doubtful if a breach is intended to discharge the insurer from all liability under the policy (as spelled out under section 33(3) of the Marine Insurance Act 1906).

However, issues of causal connection can arise for exclusion terms as well as for warranties. There were cases within the sample in which the FOS overturned an insurer's decision to reject a claim, where the breach the insurer relied on did not cause the loss in question.

In Case 42, the complainant claimed for a stolen bicycle, but the firm rejected the claim because at the time of the theft it was not locked to a secure structure. The complainant argued that this would not have made any difference: many bicycles were stolen at the same time, including locked bicycles. The ombudsman ordered the firm to pay the claim, commenting:

> The Insurance Conduct of Business (ICOB) rules state that an insurer should not refuse to meet a claim as a result of a breach of warranty or condition, unless the circumstances of the claim are connected with the breach.
>
> Although the firm is relying on an exclusion to reject this claim, it is no different to a warranty in that it requires the complainant to do something to ensure that the cover

applies. As I do not believe the lock would have made any difference, I am satisfied that the complainant has provided sufficient evidence to establish that his failure to lock his bicycle was not connected to his claim.

Case 8 concerned a travel policy that excluded pre-existing medical conditions. The complainant had to cut short her holiday when her mother suffered a heart attack, but the insurer rejected her curtailment claim on the grounds that her mother had a pre-existing medical condition. The evidence showed that her mother had suffered from hypertension for the last 50 years, but her condition appeared to be stable and controlled.

The ombudsman upheld the complaint and required the insurer to pay the claim. He commented that the insurers had provided no evidence to show that the longstanding hypertension caused the heart attack. An internet article suggesting a general link between the two was not enough. I do not consider that the firm is able to demonstrate on the balance of probabilities that [the mother's] pre-existing medical condition was directly responsible for the cardiac arrest.

The decision is noteworthy, as it goes further than the recommendations in the 1980 report. First, it puts the burden of proof firmly on the insurer to show the causal connection. Secondly, it requires the insurers to show more than a statistical correlation between hypertension and heart attacks. Instead the insurer is required to prove that the pre-existing condition is directly responsible for the event which gives rise to a claim.

Issues of Reasonable Expectation and Transparency

It was relatively rare for ombudsmen to refer explicitly to the Unfair Terms in Consumer Contract Regulations in their decisions. Among the 50 cases we looked at, the regulations were mentioned in only two. Neither of these cases was directly relevant to the issues discussed here.

However, we found several cases in which the ombudsman refused to uphold an exclusion clause contained within the policy small print, if it undermined consumers' reasonable expectation and was not brought specifically to the consumer's attention.

In his 1990 report, the Insurance Ombudsman stated that he would apply the spirit of the Unfair Contract Terms Act 1977 to cases brought to the Insurance Ombudsman Bureau. FOS continues this tradition. This also reflects the requirement in ICOB Rule 5 that significant or unusual exclusions should be brought to the consumer's attention. When a term undermines consumers' reasonable expectations, the FOS is likely to regard it as significant or unusual. Ombudsmen will be reluctant to uphold such a term unless the insurer made sufficient efforts to bring it to the consumer's attention.

This is particularly important if insurers wish to require policyholders to install a particular security measure, or to exclude claims arising "indirectly" from an existing medical condition. Such terms are not generally considered to conform to consumers' reasonable expectations, and insurers are required to take additional measures to ensure that consumers know about them. For example:

(1) In Case 43, the policy required that "high value caravans" should have an alarm. The ombudsman held that it was not made sufficiently clear to the complainants that their £9,000 caravan would be classified as high value. It was not enough to include the requirement in the policy document. Instead, such an important term should be brought to the policyholder's attention before the contract was concluded.

(2) In Case 29, the complainant declared that her husband suffered from hypertension, diabetes and gout, and received notification that these were excluded from the travel policy. When her husband suffered a heart attack on holiday, the insurers relied on policy wording excluding any claim arising "directly or indirectly" from the pre-existing condition. The ombudsman pointed to discrepancies between the policy wording and the other documents the complainant had been sent, commenting: If the firm intends to exclude claims that arise "indirectly" from any medical condition, this is a very significant restriction on cover and I consider the firm must make its meaning abundantly clear.

In this case, it was fair and reasonable that the insurers should pay the claim.

Case 14 concerned a critical illness policy offering a defined sum in the event of a heart attack. A policy term defined "heart attack" as "the death of a proportion of heart muscle as a result of inadequate blood supply", as evidenced by three symptoms: chest pain; "electrocardiograph changes"; and raised cardiac enzymes.

The complainant was diagnosed and treated for a heart attack involving pain and elevated enzymes, but which did not show changes on an ECG. The insurers refused the claim on the grounds that one of the essential elements of the definition was not met.

The ombudsman pointed out that neither the key features document nor the headline illness highlighted that a heart attack was only covered if it was of a certain severity or if it involved satisfying a three-limb test.

When a definition significantly restricts the meaning of the headline illness in a way that is inconsistent with either a policyholder's or a doctor's reasonable understanding of when a critical illness or event has occurred, then I consider it would be unfair of a firm to rely on a narrow interpretation of a definition to defeat an otherwise valid claim. In my judgment, the complainant's claim should be met because it falls within the spirit of what the policy was designed to cover and how it was sold.

It is worth noting that the FOS will be prepared to strike down a narrow definition of the risk contained within the policy small print if this was not in accordance with reasonable expectations and was not made clear to the consumer.

9

EVALUATION OF THE PRESENT POSITION

INTRODUCTION

The Law

The law on insurance warranties in general is clearly set out in the Marine Insurance Act 1906. The Act states that warranties must be exactly complied with, whether material to the risk or not. A breach cannot be remedied, but automatically discharges the insurer from liability from that date.

By including a "basis of the contract clause" in the proposal form, the insurer may convert every answer given by the proposer into a warranty. This means that any mistake discharges the insurer from all liability under the contract from the outset, even if the mistake is innocent and immaterial to the risk.

The Problems

The provisions of the Marine Insurance Act have the potential to lead to unfair results. They mean that insurers may refuse to pay a claim for actions or omissions that:

(1) *are immaterial to the risk*. For example, an insurer may refuse to pay a claim because the insured

innocently said that a lorry was kept at the wrong address, even though this did not increase the risk.

(2) *are only relevant to other risks.* For example, a failure to employ watchmen may discharge an insurer from liability for a storm claim.

(3) *have already been remedied.* For example, once a ship has entered an excluded zone, it remains uninsured even if it leaves that zone as soon as possible.

The problems are exacerbated by the use of basis of the contract clauses. Proposers are unlikely to appreciate the legal effect of a clause giving warranty status to all the answers given on a proposal form.

In 1980 the Law Commission described these results as wrong and unjust. We agree. They are wrong because they do not accord with policyholders' reasonable expectations. If a proposer has given incorrect information but the true position does not alter the risk or reduces it, the policyholder may well not realise that the policy is ineffective. If a policyholder is slow in repairing a fire alarm, they may well think that their fire cover is suspended while the problem persists. However, those unfamiliar with the niceties of insurance law are unlikely to think that this also invalidates their flood cover. Nor are they likely to realise that they will continue without fire insurance after the alarm has been fixed.

Insurers have told us that they would rarely apply the strict letter of the law. They would not, for example, refuse to pay a claim because of a breach that had already been remedied before the loss. It is difficult to know how many claims are turned down each year for breaches of terms that are not causally connected to the loss. Our own small survey of complaints brought to the FOS does not suggest that the practice is widespread, though we note that the FSA reports cases where it has occurred. The case for reform does not depend on evidence of widespread abuse. If insurers no longer think that the Marine Insurance Act 1906 embodies fair principles, this is itself strong evidence that the law should be brought into line with acceptable practice.

In the rest of this part we deal first with basis of the contract clauses, which cause the same problem in all types of insurance. We then consider specific warranties of fact or future conduct.

BASIS OF THE CONTRACT CLAUSES

In our first Issues Paper on Misrepresentation and Non-disclosure we said that basis of the contract clauses should no longer be effective to convert a statement of fact into a warranty in any kind of insurance.

Although judges have severely criticised the use of basis of contract clauses for the last 150 years, their use has been consistently upheld. In 1996 the Court of Session justified them on the grounds that the parties are free to agree what they like.9 We find this unconvincing. In most cases the insured's signature at the bottom of the proposal form containing a clause stating that "this proposal shall be the basis of the contract between us and the insurers" would not represent a true agreement because the proposer will have no idea of the implications of the statement. An insurer may have good reasons for making cover dependent on particular facts but, if so, it must make this clear to the insured.

The FSA rules (unlike the Statements of Practice they replaced) do not cover basis of the contract clauses, and in any event they are geared primarily to regulation, not to the rights of the individual insured. No doubt the FOS would take a dim view of an insurer who tried to rely on a basis of the contract clause, but as we noted in our first

Issues Paper, not all cases can be resolved by the FOS. There is a need for legislation.

At the first working seminar, there seemed to be a widespread consensus that basis of the contract clauses should be rendered ineffective in consumer insurance. There was also considerable support for our argument that they should not be effective in business insurance. However, there was some doubt about our proposal to render them totally ineffective while still permitting the parties to a business policy to vary the rules on when a policy could be avoided for misrepresentation.

SPECIFIC WARRANTIES OF FACT OR FUTURE CONDUCT

How far the injustices inherent in the law on specific warranties of fact or of future conduct have been ameliorated. We saw that because of the Unfair Terms in Consumer Contracts Regulations 1999, and the existence of the FSA regulations and the FOS scheme, the position in consumer insurance is different to that in business insurance. Therefore we consider warranties in consumer insurance before we turn to warranties in business insurance.

Consumer Insurance

The Unfair Terms in Consumer Regulations

The 1993 Directive and the Unfair Terms in Consumer Contracts Regulations 1999 protect consumer insureds against the effect of unfair terms. The regulations are not widely understood, and appear not to have been used to their full potential in insurance cases that fall within the topics covered in this Issues Paper.

We have shown that they can be used to challenge warranties, descriptions of the risk and other forms of exclusion that are either not made obvious to the proposer (for example because the term is just one among many in the small print) or whose meaning or requirements are not clear. The terms will be open to challenge on the grounds of unfairness unless they are part of the "definition of the main subject matter" and are in plain, intelligible language. We have argued that they cannot be part of the main subject matter unless they are substantially in line with what the consumer reasonably expected. In other words, the insurer must take reasonable steps to ensure the consumer is aware of warranties, descriptions of the risk and other forms of exclusion. Simply including the warranty or exclusion in the contract documents is not enough.

The effect of the Regulations is not as clear as it should be. The two Law Commissions have already made recommendations to rewrite the Regulations in a clearer and more accessible way, so that the implications behind the Directive are made explicit. The recommendations have been accepted in principle, subject to a regulatory impact assessment. We believe that if our draft bill were implemented, what is required of insurers would be made significantly clearer.

A consumer may be aware of the existence of a warranty but unaware of its implications. A consumer may realise that the insurer requires certain locks, but not realise that a failure to install these locks discharges the insurer from liability for flooding. We have argued that the Regulations are very likely to apply to a clause making a term into a warranty if it does not set out the insurer's rights should the warranty be broken, because its effects will almost always be substantially different from what the consumer reasonably expects. Then it is open to the court to hold the term unfair because it would give the insurer the right to treat itself as discharged for a breach that was immaterial, or where there was no causal link between the breach and the loss for which the claim was made.

However, we do not think that in practice the problem for consumers has been solved by the Regulations. We think that it is important that consumers are protected by a firm rule, that a breach of warranty should not absolve the insurer from liability if the breach was immaterial or there was no causal connection between it and the claim. The consumer should not be required to make the complex and difficult argument that the term permitting this first is not a core term and secondly is unfair.

The FSA Rules

Is reform of the law along these lines needed? ICOB Rule 7.3.6 currently states that "except where there is evidence of fraud" the insurer may not refuse to meet a claim for a breach of warranty or condition "unless the circumstances of the claim are connected with the breach". However, the FSA rule suffers from two problems.

First, the FSA rule permits an insurer to refuse to pay a claim where there is inconclusive evidence of fraud. This effectively allows insurers to substitute their own opinion for that of the court. While inconclusive evidence of fraud may be a reason for excusing the insurer from a regulatory sanction, it is not a ground on which the insurer should be entitled to reject an individual claim where the breach of warranty and the claim had no causal connection.

It could be argued that insurers should have some discretion not to pay claims where they have robust evidence that nevertheless falls short of proof. We will return to the definition and proof of fraud in a subsequent paper.

However, we do not think that the problem insurers have in proving fraud is a good reason for permitting them to retain technical or unmeritorious defences to paying claims. Suppose for example, an insurer suspects (but cannot prove) that a policyholder has inflated the costs of repair following storm damage. If the insurer refused the claim because the burglar alarm was not working, it could undermine trust on both sides. The insured would be unable to defend themselves on the substance of the charge, while the insurer would not have established the substance of the wrongdoing.

Secondly, the FSA rule does not give the insured a ready remedy. In a private law contract claim, the court would be required to find for the insurer on the basis of strict law. The consumer may then have a claim to damages for breach of statutory duty under section 150(1) on the ground that the insurer should not have taken the point. However, it is difficult to reconcile this with the strict legal position that an insurer is automatically discharged from liability with no need for further action on its part. It is odd to think that an insurer may be sued for damages for failing to pay a claim for which it is not liable. It must be asked whether any consumer insured would understand the position, let alone actually make a claim.

The Financial Ombudsman Service

Our research did not reveal a case directly on the need for a causal connection between a loss and a breach of warranty. However the case of the stolen bicycle described earlier (which involved an exception rather than a warranty) shows that the Ombudsmen would almost certainly insist that the insurer pay the claim.

We do not think that the existence of the FOS scheme is a sufficient reason for leaving the law as it is, however. The reason is just the same as in other cases we have considered. Not all cases will reach the FOS; and it makes no sense to have different rules for the courts on the one hand and the FOS on the other. This incoherence and complexity alone is a good reason for reform.

CONCLUSION

It is our conclusion that although the UTCCR, the FSA Rules and the FOS offer valuable protection to consumer insureds in relation to breaches of warranty, there is a clear need for reform of the underlying law in consumer insurance cases.

Business Insurance

The problems with the law on breach of warranty are not confined to consumer insureds. We do not think it accords with the expectation of any class of insureds that the insurer should be discharged by an immaterial breach of warranty, or one that has been cured before any claim arose. Nor would policyholders expect a claim to be rejected on the ground of a breach of warranty that had no connection to the loss. We discuss below whether the parties should be able to agree expressly that a breach of warranty should have such consequences. However, we do not think that this should be the "default" rule for breach of warranty (that is the rule that will apply if nothing different is provided in the contract).

Neither the FSA rules nor UTCCR cover businesses. For insured businesses, their only protection lies in inviting the court to construe a term to give it a fair meaning. The courts are often prepared to do this, sometimes finding ambiguities in the words used, even when the words appear firm and clear.

However, we do not think that it is an adequate substitute for law reform. The process of reinterpreting the effect of contractual terms can cause considerable complexity and difficulty, as is shown by the case law on whether a notification clause can be an innominate term. And in some cases the courts are prepared to give terms their traditional (harsh) meaning.

The problems caused by the harshness of the law can affect any business, but they appear most severe for small and medium businesses. They may not understand the import of words such as "warranty" and, even if they do, they lack the bargaining position to change the insurer's standard wording. Furthermore, they are particularly vulnerable to legal uncertainty as they lack the legal knowledge and resources to argue cases before the courts. Insurers may therefore be able to use the harshness of the law as set out in the MIA 1906 as a negotiating tool.

Large businesses are more able to protect themselves. They have the resources to understand the issues, and the bargaining position to renegotiate terms. We were told, for example, that one large company refuses to agree to warranties in any circumstances. This does not suggest, however, that reform is unnecessary for large businesses. Rather it suggests that all businesses might benefit from the change we are proposing. The fact that businesses which are able to do so exclude the rule, and presumably pay any resulting increase in premium, suggests that it is a poor rule in the first place. We conclude that the law on breach of warranty requires reform in all types of insurance. The question is exactly what shape the reform should take.

10

WARRANTIES IN OTHER JURISDICTIONS

The notion of a warranty that has the effect prescribed by the Marine Insurance Act 1906 is unique to the common law. Many civil lawyers express astonishment at the idea that insurers can avoid liability for trivial breaches of obligations, even if the breach has been remedied or is unconnected with the loss. However, Australia, New Zealand and Canada built their insurance law on English common law principles, as set out in the Marine Insurance Act and its Commonwealth variants.

Below we begin by considering Australia and New Zealand. Both have attempted to correct the perceived defects in the law by legislation, and there are direct lessons to be learnt from their experience. We then look briefly at Canada, where the task of mitigating the harshness of the law has been left to the courts. In the USA, insurance law is largely a matter for each state. Some, such as Texas, have introduced legislation to require a causal connection between the breach and the loss. We conclude with a short comparison with the civil law approach.

AUSTRALIA AND NEW ZEALAND

Both Australia and New Zealand faced similar problems to the UK. They started with the same common law principles, and both reformed their law by statute within five years of the Law Commission's 1980 report. New Zealand passed the Insurance Law Reform Act in 1977; Australia passed the Insurance Contracts Act in 1984. To some extent the various reforms influenced each other: the Law Commission's working paper refers to the New Zealand reform, while the Australian Law Reform Commission's 1982 report discusses the English Law Commission's recommendations in depth. The Law Commission's draft bill, the New Zealand Act and the Australian Act approach the same issues in slightly different ways, and therefore provide interesting commentaries on each other.

We look first at provisions to abolish basis of the contract clauses and then at the need for a causal connection between the breach of warranty and the loss. Finally we consider procedural requirements to bring terms to the notice of the insured.

Abolishing Basis of the Contract clauses New Zealand

The Insurance Law Reform Act 1977 prevents insurers from using basis of the contract clauses to avoid liability for non-material representations made in proposal forms or other pre-contractual documentation.

Different rules apply to life insurance and other types of insurance, with the life insurance rules offering the insured greater protection. For general insurance, the insurer may avoid at any time, but only for representations that are substantially incorrect and material. For life policies, there is an additional requirement that, unless the misrepresentation is made fraudulently, the insurer can only avoid in the first three years.

The life provisions are set out:

(1) A life policy shall not be avoided by reason only of any statement (other than a statement as to the age

of the life insured) made in any proposal or other document on the faith of which the policy was issued, reinstated, or renewed by the company unless the statement—

(a) Was substantially incorrect; and

(b) Was material; and

(c) Was made either—

(i) Fraudulently; or

(ii) Within the period of 3 years immediately preceding the date on which the policy is sought to be avoided or the date of the death of the life insured, whichever is the earlier.

(2) For the purposes of subparagraph (i) of paragraph (c) of subsection

(i) of this section, a statement is made fraudulently if the person making it makes it—

(a) Knowing it is incorrect; or

(b) Without belief in its correctness; or

(c) Recklessly, without caring whether it is correct or not.

Section covers other types of insurance contracts:

(1) A contract of insurance shall not be avoided by reason only of any statement made in any proposal or other document on the faith of which the contract was entered into, reinstated, or renewed by the insurer unless the statement

(a) Was substantially incorrect; and

(b) Was material.

(1) ... a statement is substantially incorrect only if the difference between what is stated and

what is actually correct would have been considered material by a prudent insurer.

(2) ... a statement is material only if that statement would have influenced

the judgment of a prudent insurer in fixing the premium or in determining whether he would have taken or continued the risk upon substantially the same terms.

In a 1982 case, the judge explained that the purpose behind sections 5 and 6 was to alleviate the harshness and artificiality resulting from the common practice of insurers requiring proponents to warrant the complete accuracy of all answers to questions put by insurers, with the result that any inaccuracy, whether by way of positive misstatement or omission, and whether major or trivial, material or immaterial to risk or loss, voided the policy.

Tarr and Kennedy comment that,

The combined effect of these sections meant that an insurer could only avoid a policy when the difference between what was stated in the proposal and what was actually correct would have been considered material by a prudent insurer and would have influenced that insurer's judgment in fixing the premium or determining whether he or she would have taken or continued the risk upon substantially the same terms.

Australia

The Australian Law Reform Commission (ALRC) recommended substantial changes to the law on non-disclosure and misrepresentation. It was concerned that an insurer may seek to evade these recommendations by converting any statement into a warranty of existing fact. Consequently, it argued that "all warranties of existing fact should be treated as representations".

This recommendation has been implemented in section 24 of the Insurance Contracts Act 1984: A statement made in or in connection with a contract of insurance, being a statement made by or attributable to the insured, with respect to the existence of a state of affairs does not have effect as a warranty but has effect as though it were a statement made to the insurer by the insured during the negotiations for the contract but before it was entered into.

This renders 'basis of the contract' clauses of no effect where the statement is about existing facts, as opposed to promises about the future.

The policy behind section 24 would appear to be similar to the policy behind Clause 9 of the Law Commission's draft Bill, though the wording is simpler and more all embracing. It covers all statements of current fact, not just those made in answer to pre-set questions. It would also cover specific statements made in the policy itself.

CONCLUSION

Given the level of criticisms of basis of the contract clauses, it is not surprising that both New Zealand and Australia have enacted provisions to abolish them. Such reform would also appear to be necessary to prevent evasion of any changes to the law of misrepresentation in insurance contracts.

We are not aware that either provision has caused problems. Abolishing basis of the contract clauses would appear to be practicable, and there are several legislative models to choose from in drafting appropriate provisions. A causal connection between the breach and the loss

Both New Zealand and Australia have enacted provisions to curb the insurers right to avoid liability for a breach of warranty if the policyholder is able to prove that the breach did not cause or contribute to the loss.

The first thing to note about these reforms is that they apply to all terms which exclude or limit liability – not just to warranties. As the ALRC put it, "the form in which the insurer seeks to protect itself from an increase in risk should not be allowed to affect the extent of that protection". It said that its recommendations should extend not only to strict warranties and other terms imposing obligations on the insured, but also to exclusions from cover of certain risks. Were they not to extend to temporal exclusions, legislation based on the present recommendations might be avoided simply by rephrasing an obligation ("the insured warrants that the car will be kept in a roadworthy condition") as a temporal exclusion ("the insurer will not be liable while the car is in an unroadworthy condition"). The legislation might also be avoided if obligations and exclusions were omitted and the cover itself stated in such a way as to achieve the same ends ("cover is granted in respect of the roadworthy car").

The New Zealand and Australian provisions have a common core. However, the Australian Act goes further than the New Zealand one, and provides an additional level of protection for policyholders.

New Zealand

The Insurance Law Reform Act 1977 forbids certain exclusions. Section 11 states:

Where –

(a) By the provisions of a contract of insurance the circumstances in which the insurer is bound to indemnify the insured against loss are so defined as to exclude or limit the liability of the insurer to indemnify the insured on the happening of certain events or on the existence of certain circumstances; and

(b) In the view of the court or arbitrator determining the claim of the insured the liability of the insurer has been so defined because the happening of such events or the existence of such circumstances was in the view of the insurer likely to increase the risk of such loss occurring,-the insured shall not be disentitled to be indemnified by the insurer by reason only of such provisions of the contract of insurance if the insured proves on the balance of probability that the loss in respect of which the insured seeks to be indemnified was not caused or contributed to by the happening of such events or the existence of such circumstances.

In *Barnaby v South British Insurance Co,* Hardie Boys J explained the effect of the section as follows:

The key to this section is to be found in the last words of para. (b): the section is designed to deal with those kinds of exclusion clauses which provide for circumstances likely to increase the risk of a loss which the policy actually covers. The most common examples are found in the field of motor vehicle insurance, such as driving a motor vehicle whilst under the influence of alcohol, or driving a motor vehicle while it is in an unsafe condition. The section is not designed to deal with exclusion clauses which specify the kind of loss or the quantum of loss to which the cover does not apply at all.

It has been accepted that section 11 applies to promissory warranties. However, insurers may still avoid a policy for a breach of warranty before a loss occurs, and this has been criticised by academics.

Section 11 is more generous to the policyholder than the test suggested in the Law Commission's 1980 draft Bill. This is because the New Zealand test allows the insured to recover if they prove that the loss was "not caused or contributed to" by the breach. By contrast, the English recommendation would require the insured to prove that the breach "could not have increased the risk that the event... would occur". The Australian Law Reform Commission explain the difference in the following example: Suppose, for example, that a motor vehicle has been modified in breach of a warranty. The breach increases the risk of a malfunction of the vehicle's brake system. An accident occurs which is entirely the fault of a driver in not keeping a proper look-out. The brakes are applied too late but function admirably.

The ALRC suggest that although the breach did not cause or contribute to the loss, the insured could not prove that the breach did not increase the risk that the loss would occur in the way it did in fact occur.

Australia

The ALRC dealt with these problems by recommending a two-part test. The causation test would only apply to provisions that could reasonably be regarded as capable of causing or contributing to the loss for which insurance cover was provided. For other breaches, a proportionality test would be applied, allowing the insurer to reduce its liability "by the amount that fairly represents the extent to which... [its] interests were prejudiced".

The ALRC also recommended greater protection to policyholders than the New Zealand Act provides where the breach caused only part of the loss. Here the insurer would still be liable for the part of the loss that was not caused by the insured's act.

Suppose, for example, a site owner has two buildings: Building A, where the sprinkler system has been maintained, and Building B, where it has not. If fire spreads from Building A to Building B, the insurer would still be liable to meet the loss to Building A.

These recommendations were enacted in section 54 of the Insurance Contracts Act 1984:

(1) Subject to this section, where the effect of a contract of insurance would, but for this section, be that the insurer may refuse to pay a claim, either in whole or in part, by reason of some act of the insured or of some other person, being an act that occurred after the contract was entered into but not being an act in respect of which sub-section (2) applies, the insurer may not refuse to pay the claim by reason only of that act but the insurer's liability in respect of the claim is reduced by the amount that fairly represents the extent to which the insurer's interests were prejudiced as a result of that act.

(2) Subject to the succeeding provisions of this section, where the act could reasonably be regarded as being capable of causing or contributing to a loss in respect of which insurance cover is provided by the contract, the insurer may refuse to pay the claim.

(3) Where the insured proves that no part of the loss that gave rise to the claim was caused by the act, the insurer may not refuse to pay the claim by reason only of the act.

(4) Where the insured proves that some part of the loss that gave rise to the claim was not caused by the act, the insurer may not refuse to pay the claim, so far as it concerns that part of the loss, by reasons only of the act.

(5) Where –

(a) The act was necessary to protect the safety of a person or to preserve property; or

(b) It was not reasonably possible for the insured or other person not to do the act, the insurer may not refuse to pay the claim by reason only of the act.

(6) A reference in this section to an act includes a reference to –

(a) An omission; and

(b) An act or omission that has the effect of altering the state or condition of the subject-matter of the contract or of allowing the state or condition of that subject matter to alter.

SECTION 54 IN PRACTICE

This section has caused considerable litigation.9 The main difficulty lies in the ALRC's desire to extend protection beyond clauses which impose obligations on policyholders, to those which limit the scope of the cover (as in the example where cover is granted only "in respect of the roadworthy car"). This has led to considerable debate about how far section 54 can be used to extend policies to cover risks outside the scope of the policy the insurer had written.

An example is *Kelly v New Zealand Insurance Co Ltd*, which concerned a home and contents policy.10 Here the insured could have extended their cover by providing the insurer with a list of specified items, but chose not to do so. The question was whether this amounted to an omission within the terms of section 54(6), which (but for the section) would permit the insurer to refuse to pay.

The Supreme Court of Western Australia drew a distinction between an "omission" and an "inaction". This, they said, was an inaction, whereby the insured exercised their right not to expand the scope of the cover. Therefore the section did not apply.

However, in *Antico v Heath Fielding Australia Pty Ltd*, the High Court reached the opposite conclusion.11 This case concerned legal expenses insurance, where indemnity was conditional upon the insurer consenting to defend the claim. The policyholder failed to obtain consent, and the question was whether this amounted to an omission, which could be excused under section 54. The High Court found that section 54 applied: the word "omission" did just refer to a failure to discharge an obligation, but also included "a failure to exercise a right, choice or liberty which the insured enjoys under the contract of insurance".

However, most of the litigation about section 54 has been about "claims made and notified policies". These policies are common in the professional indemnity market, and are a way in which insurers protect themselves against long-tailed claims that may not arise for many years after the policy has been issued. Typically, a "claims made" policy only applies if the claim is made during the period of cover. A "claims made and notified policy" usually extends cover to claims made after cover has ceased, provided that the claim arises from an occurrence which has been notified to the insurer during the relevant period. It is common for such policies to include a deeming clause, stating that where the facts have been notified to the insurer within the period of insurance it is deemed to be a claim made during the policy period.

There have been a series of cases in which policyholders failed to notify the insurer of an occurrence during the relevant period. Policyholders have argued that this failure amounts to an omission within the terms of section 54(6) and that the section offers them protection. The leading case is the High Court's decision in *FAI v Australian Hospital Care Pty Ltd.*14 Here, the professional indemnity policy contained a deeming clause of the sort described above. The insured had been aware of facts giving rise to an injury during the period of cover, but had not notified the insurer because it did not expect that a claim would be made. It argued that this omission could be cured by section 54. To the alarm of the insurance industry, the High Court found for the insured. The Court drew a distinction between "an inherently essential element of the claim" (where section 54 does not apply) and other ancillary or procedural matters (where it does apply). Where the demand must be made within the period, or where the insured must become aware of facts within the period – and these requirements have not been met-the claim does not fall within the policy. No relief can be given. However, here the failure to notify was a procedural matter, and the relief applied.

An added twist to these difficulties is that under section 40 of the Insurance Contracts Act 1982 a "claims made policy" is deemed to be a "a claims made and notified policy". The statute states that the insurer must pay where the insured gave notice in writing to an insurer of the facts that might give rise to the claim. Section 54 goes one step further by opening up the possibility that claims must be paid even if the facts are *not* notified. The combined effect of sections 40 and 54 has made it difficult for professional indemnity insurers to limit their liability for long-tailed claims, and there have been extensive calls for reform.

That said, it is possible to exaggerate the difficulties associated with section 54. First, even if the section applies, it does not necessarily require that the claim is paid. The claim may be reduced by an amount which "fairly represents the extent to which the insurer's interests were prejudiced" as a result of the act or omission. In *Ferrcom Pty Ltd v Commercial Union Assurance Co of Australia*, the High Court found that the prejudice to the insurer was equivalent to its entire liability. The owners of a mobile crane had failed to notify the insurer that there had been a change of circumstances, and that the crane was now registered to be driven on public roads. The court found that if the insurer had been told it would have exercised its right to cancel the policy and would not have been liable to meet any subsequent claim.

Secondly, in 2003 the Commonwealth Treasury Review of the section commented that "not a single stakeholder has sought the removal of section 54". It found that the section worked satisfactorily in relation to the vast majority of occurrence insurance, and "the prominent message from meetings and submissions is that the operation of section 54 in relation to 'occurrence' policies should remain unchanged". The review recommended reform only in relation to "claims made" and "claims made and notified" policies.

THE ALRC REVIEW OF MARINE INSURANCE

The 1982 Act did not cover marine insurance. In 2001, the ALRC considered whether similar reforms should be introduced for marine insurance. The Commission concluded that as currently drafted, section 54 went too far to be suitable to the marine area. In important respects, its practical effect was "to allow the insured to unilaterally alter the bargain made by the parties, arguably to the extent of fundamentally changing the scope of the insurance". The degree of discretion involved in assessing the extent of prejudice the insurer had suffered allowed too much room for dispute.

Subsection (4) could also introduce unacceptable uncertainty. This allows "some part of the loss" to be paid where the insured proves that that act did not cause that part of the loss. The ALRC commented that "this approach may lead to practical difficulties in quantifying an insurer's liability", and could increase the cost of litigating disputes.

Despite these problems, however, the ALRC found a wide consensus that marine warranties could operate in a harsh and unfair manner. The Queensland Commercial

Fishermen's Organisation were particularly concerned, and instrumental in prompting the review. Even submissions from insurers expressed considerable support for reform.

The Review concluded that an insurer should only be discharged from liability as a result of a breach of the insured's obligations, if the loss was caused by the breach. Otherwise the remedy should lie in damages.

In some ways, the ALRC thought that section 54 did not go far enough. Section 54 talks about acts "causing or contributing to a loss", which could cover any situation where there was a connection between breach and loss. The ALRC thought that the test should require "proximate causation", which is a well understood insurance law concept, and more generous to the insured.

For these reasons the ALRC recommended that the amended MIA should permit the parties to include a term that the insurer is discharged from liability to indemnify the insured for loss proximately caused by a breach by the insured of an express term of the contract. An express term providing for the insurer's discharge from liability could be drafted to apply to the insured's obligations generally or only to particular breaches. In the absence of such a term, breach of the contract will entitle the insurer only to such relief as may be available under the general law of contract, which would generally be the award of damages.

In both Australia and New Zealand there is a consensus that insurers should not be permitted to avoid liability for breaches of insurance terms that are unrelated to the loss. This consensus has endured, despite some serious problems with the way that section 54 has been drafted.

There does not appear to be a problem with drafting legislation to deal with terms where "the happening of such events or the existence of such circumstances was in the view of the insurer likely to increase the risk of such loss occurring". In these circumstances, it is possible to provide that the policy should not be avoided where the breach did not in fact increase the risk, or cause the loss. These provisions have secured acceptance within the industry.

The problems appear where the legislation goes wider than this, to cover acts or omissions that do not increase the risk of a loss occurring, such as notification clauses. It is often difficult to distinguish conceptually between an omission and the absence of a central element of the claim. If provisions are drafted widely to deal with all potential evasion techniques, they may permit the insured to argue that the cover they receive should extend beyond the cover they have bought. Procedural requirements to bring terms to the notice of the insured

One problem with the existing law is that terms may be strictly enforced even if the insured was not fully aware of them. The Law Commission's draft Bill therefore included a requirement that the policyholder should be given a written statement of a warranty at or before the contract was entered into, or as soon as practicable thereafter. The difficulty with this proposal is that just because a term is in writing does not mean that it is clear or understandable, or even brought to the policyholder's attention.

We have not been able to find any general procedural requirements in New Zealand (although their 1985 Act does require insurers to disclose the existence and effect of a clause imposing pro rata averaging).

In Australia, the ALRC wrestled with the problem. How does one ensure that the important terms are brought to policyholders' attention, without burying them in reading matter? Their solution was to prescribe standard cover for the five main types of consumer policies: motor, householder, personal accident, consumer credit and travel. These terms would be set out in regulations, after consultation with the industry. Insurers would be free to market policies that offered less than the standard cover. But if so, they would be required to draw the policyholder's attention to every respect in which the policy offered less than the standard. We have not yet been able to find how these recommendations have worked in practice.

Prescribed standard cover is common in the USA and in several European jurisdictions. However, it has some weaknesses. It does not ensure that consumers are aware of their policy terms, as most consumers will not know what the standard terms provide. Terms may become known over time, but if policies are to keep pace with changes in the market, even standard terms will need to change frequently. The process of prescribing and updating terms adds to the regulatory burden, as every change will require insurers to adapt their contractual and marketing documents. Insurers also object that their marketing effort is required to concentrate on the negative – what is not covered, rather than what is.

CANADA

In other Commonwealth jurisdictions, the problem of warranties has been tackled by the courts rather than the legislature. As Lord Hobhouse said in *The Star Sea*: It is a striking feature of this branch of the law that other legal systems are increasingly discarding the more extreme features of English law which allow an insurer to avoid liability on grounds which do not relate to the occurrence of the loss.

In Canada, the Marine Insurance Act 1993 is based on the UK Marine Insurance Act 1906. However courts have limited it "to situations where the warranty is material to the risk and the breach has a bearing on the loss." Where cases do not meet this criterion, the courts tend to find that the clause is not a true warranty at all.

The Bamcell II

The leading case is the Supreme Court decision in *Century Insurance Company of Canada v Case Existological Laboratories Ltd. ("The Bamcell II")*. The Bamcell II was a converted barge used for oceanographic experiments. The owners had negotiated a policy, which included the following term Warranted that a watchman is stationed on board the BAMCELL II each night from 2200 hours to 0600 hours with instructions for shutting down all equipment in an emergency.

In fact, the owners never placed a watchman on board. However, there were no problems at night. The loss occurred mid afternoon, and therefore the breach had "absolutely no bearing whatever on the loss". As a result, Ritchie J held: The clause would only have been effective if the loss had occurred between 2200 hours and 0600 hours, and it was proved that there was no watchman stationed aboard during those hours. To this extent the condition contained in the clause constituted a limitation of the risk insured against but it was not a warranty.

Soyer argues that on the facts there was a clear intention that the term should be a warranty. He thinks the English courts would have regarded it as an express warranty. This is an open question. Some cases suggest that the English courts may take an approach which is similar to the Canadian one. For example, in *Kler Knitwear v Lombard,* Mr Justice Morland cited *Bamcell II* and used it to justify overriding the clear words of the policy. However, this decision is only at first instance and it has been subjected to academic criticism. The English courts also tend to construe marine insurance contracts more strictly.

The reasoning in *Bamcell II* and *Kler Knitwear* is predicated on the existence of some ambiguity in the term, which is construed against the insurer. It is difficult to know how far the Canadian court will go in overriding unambiguous words simply to achieve fair outcomes. Soyer quotes the British Columbia Builders' Risk Clauses as an example of insurers' attempts to prevent the courts from applying *Bamcell II* to reinterpret warranties as descriptions of risk. Clause 1 is as unambiguous as possible: This policy contains warranties and general conditions none of which are to be interpreted as suspensive conditions. The Underwriters have agreed to accept the risk of insuring the Vessel on the condition precedent that the Assured will comply strictly and literally with these warranties and conditions. If the Assured breaches any of these warranties or conditions, the Underwriters at their option will not pay any claims arising thereafter, regardless of whether or not breach is causative or in any way connected to such claim.

It is not clear how the courts would deal with a *Bamcell II* type case in the light of such clear, definite and unambiguous wording.

As we have seen, the English courts have gone some way to temper the unfairness associated with the strict application of warranties, and these developments have been taken further by the Canadian Supreme Court. Although these developments prevent unjust decisions, they also introduce some uncertainty and incoherence into the law. The danger is of repeated litigation, as insurers respond to court decisions by rewriting their contracts in even less ambiguous terms.

THE USA

Traditionally, US marine insurance law followed the British approach and was considered to be a federal matter.

This, however, changed in 1955 following the Supreme Court decision in the *Wilburn Boat* case.

The case concerned a small houseboat, kept on a lake between Texas and Oklahoma. The policy contained various stipulations that the policyholders had breached. Contrary to the terms of the policy, the insured had pledged the boat, carried passengers on several occasions and had at times leased the vessel. A fire destroyed the boat while it was moored, in circumstances that had nothing to do with the breaches of warranty. The insurers argued that, under Federal law, there was no need for a causal link between the breaches and the loss. The policyholders, however, argued that the matter should be dealt with under Texan law, where breaches of the policy would not defeat the claim unless they contributed to the loss. Eventually the case found its way to the Supreme Court, which held that insurance law was a matter for each state.

The case has generated considerable debate within the US: some see it as a necessary part of the state/federal balance; others as a source of uncertainty and complexity. One element behind the decision, however, may have been the Supreme Court's unhappiness with the harshness and rigidity of the English approach.

The result is that the way warranties are to be interpreted and applied is largely a matter for state law. As we have seen, some states, such as Texas, require a causal connection between the breach and the loss before permitting the insurer to avoid paying a claim.

By contrast, in New York, the requirement is that a breach of warranty will avoid an insurance contract, provided that it "materially increases the risk of loss, damage or injury within the coverage of the contract".34 If the contract specifies two or more kinds of loss (such as fire and theft) the breach will only avoid the particular kind of loss to which the warranty relates. This does not mean that the breach must cause or contribute to the specific loss, but it must be such that would materially increase the risk of a loss of the same sort. In other words, a breach of a burglar alarm condition would not affect a fire claim, but it would avoid a theft policy, so as to permit the insurer to refuse a claim for theft, however the thieves had entered the building.

CIVIL LAW JURISDICTIONS

UK law on breach of warranty diverges from that of most other European States, which require that a breach be causally connected to the loss in some way before it can absolve the insurer from payment.

Baris Soyer provides a detailed analysis of the English, German and Norwegian approach to breach of warranty in marine insurance. He shows that in both Germany and Norway provisions exist to exempt the insurer from liability if the nature of the risk changes during the life of the policy. However, unlike the English law, these require some degree of culpability and causation.

An example will illustrate the main differences. Under German law, the insurer is not normally liable if the insured put a vessel to sea in an unseaworthy condition. But this is subject to two important limitations. First, the exemption only applies to loss caused by the conduct. If, for example, the loss was unrelated to the unseaworthiness, the insurance policy continues. Secondly, it is open to the insured to show that they were not "responsible" for the unseaworthiness-ie that it was not a deliberate or negligent act. Norwegian law is similar. By contrast, under the Marine Insurance Act 1906, voyage polices contain an implied warranty "that at the commencement of the voyage the ship shall be seaworthy for the purposes of the particular adventure insured". This means that if the ship is not seaworthy at the beginning of the voyage, all liability is avoided even if the insured is not at fault; or the defect is remedied; or the loss is totally unconnected with the defect.

Trine-Lise Wilhelmsen, a Professor at the Scandinavian Institute of Maritime Law, comments that for most people in the Civil Law world, the UK concept of a warranty is "hard to understand and even harder to explain". Although the words may seem "deceptively simple", the consequences lack "logical reason" and cannot be explained in terms of either legal fairness or economic efficiency.

John Hare, Professor of Shipping Law at the University of Cape Town is even more outspoken. He describes the Anglo-American marine insurance warranty as "a prodigal aberration from the European *ius communis* of marine insurance". He suggests that "the prodigal, in whatever systems it has raised its unwelcome head, ought to be brought back into the fold in the interests of the very fairness, justice and equity to which English law so properly aspires".

UK warranty law is inconsistent with the mandatory, but milder, provisions concerning alteration of risk in several Civil Law countries. Wilhelmsen comments that if there are to be attempts towards harmonisation, it is unlikely that many other European States will move towards the British model: The mandatory provisions in Danish and Swedish ICA concerning alteration of risk do not seem to permit the far more harsh regulation of warranties. Also the French and Italian legislations are more favourable towards the assured than the common law principle of warranties. In an attempt towards harmonisation, this implies either that the common law systems are willing to soften their regulation, or that a double set of clauses are suggested. It does not seem realistic that the legislators in the four mentioned civil law countries will open the door for the stricter principle of warranties, ref. the Norwegian political attitude on this point. Also it would seem to go backwards into the future to adopt legal principles from 1906 instead of the principles of the far more modern insurance legislation in the civil law countries.

PROVISIONAL PROPOSALS

The law on breach of warranty in the United Kingdom has the potential to cause considerable unfairness to policyholders by allowing insurers to avoid paying claims for technical reasons which are unconnected with the loss that has occurred. We think it is wrong that insurers should still be entitled to avoid liability for a breach that has already been cured: for example, a delay in inspecting sprinklers should not affect liability for a fire that occurs after the sprinklers have passed their inspection. Nor should a policy be discharged for a breach that is unconnected with the loss: failure to employ watchmen should not affect a claim for storm damage that employing the watchmen would not have prevented or reduced. At the very least these should not be the "default" rules.

"Basis of the contract" clauses are a particular mischief. They allow insurers to use a form of words that few policyholders understand to extend the protections already available to them for misrepresentation to cover answers that are not material to the risk, or are made without fraud or negligence.

Insurance is based on trust, and when insurers deny liability for inappropriate reasons it may undermine faith in the industry. It does not accord with good practice. As we have seen, it may also bring UK law into disrepute.

In the discussion that follows we distinguish between warranties of past or existing fact, and warranties about future conduct. This is because a warranty of past or existing fact already takes effect as a representation. In Issues Paper 1 we explored the remedies currently available for inaccurate representations and how we think they should be reformed. Permitting such representations to be made into warranties would have the effect of entitling insurers to additional remedies, particularly if the representation was made innocently.

Below we start by recapping the tentative proposals on reform of the law of misrepresentation and non-disclosure that we made in our first Issues Paper. We also note one change in our thinking in the light of the discussion of that paper at the seminars.

We then consider how far insurers should, in effect, be permitted additional remedies for misrepresentation, first through the use of basis of the contract clauses and secondly through specific warranties and other terms as to existing facts. We tentatively conclude not only that basis of the contract clauses should not be effective to turn all representations made by the proposer into warranties, but also that for consumer insurance, every statement of past and existing fact should be treated as a representation rather than as a warranty. This means that insurers should not be entitled to escape liability for misrepresentations that are made innocently and reasonably; and for negligent misrepresentations, the insurers' remedy should be proportionate.

For business insurance we ask whether we should follow the same approach or whether warranties as to specific facts should still be a ground on which the insurer in business insurance policies may refuse to pay a claim, and possibly treat the contract as discharged. If warranties of specific fact are to be permitted, we later argue that they should be subject to certain formal requirements (such as the warranty being set out in a schedule to the policy).

Furthermore, when the question is whether the insurer must pay a claim, the claim must be causally connected to the breach of warranty.

We then consider options for reforming warranties about future conduct. We make two tentative proposals:

(1) to be valid, a warranty of future conduct should be set out in writing;

(2) insurers should only be entitled to avoid liability to pay a claim because of a breach of warranty if the breach bears some connection with the loss.

We discuss whether a causal connection should also be required for other types of term that limit the risk, such as definitions of the risk and exceptions. We tentatively conclude that it should be required, unless it would be unreasonable for the insured to assume that it was covered by the policy at the time of the event.

We then inquire whether the reform proposals should apply to all forms of insurance. We ask whether different arguments apply first to marine, aviation and transport insurance (MAT) and then to reinsurance. Our present thinking is that the reforms should apply in these areas, though we welcome views on whether there are good reasons to treat these forms of insurance differently. Marine insurance raises particular issues about the implied warranties set out in the Marine Insurance Act (which we discuss briefly). We ask if these should be subjected to the same causal connection test that we have proposed for other warranties.

Finally, we consider the implications these reforms would have for sections 33 and 34 of the Marine Insurance Act 1906. We tentatively propose that insurance policies should no longer be discharged automatically as the result of a breach of warranty. Instead the insurer should have the option to terminate the contract for the future (without prejudice to its liability to pay any claims that have arisen already).

This raises questions about whether the insured should be entitled to a pro-rata return of any premium paid, and whether the insurer should give notice of the termination. An insurer may also lose the right to terminate an insurance contract, because they are taken to have "waived" their rights. We consider the implications for our suggested proposals for the law of waiver and affirmation.

OUR TENTATIVE PROPOSALS ON MISREPRESENTATION AND NONDISCLOSURE

All Insurance

For both consumer and business insurance we proposed that:

(1) Insurers should only be entitled to a remedy for an insured's nondisclosure or misrepresentation in so far as this is material, as defined below. The same test should apply to misrepresentation and nondisclosure.

(2) First, the actual insurer must show inducement, in that had it known the true facts it would not have entered into the same contract on the same terms or at all.

(3) Additionally, the insurer must show either

(i) that the proposer appreciated that the fact in question would be relevant to the insurer (in the sense that it would have an effect on the insurer's mind in assessing the risk) or, if not,

(ii) that a reasonable insured would have appreciated that the fact would be relevant to the insurer (in the sense set out above).

(4) In assessing what a reasonable insured would appreciate, the courts should take into account the type of policy, the way the policy was advertised and sold, and the normal characteristics of consumers in the market. However, they would not look at individual circumstances, known only to the insured.

We tentatively proposed that:

(1) Insurers should be allowed to avoid policies where the insured has acted fraudulently at the pre-contractual stage,

(2) If the insured had reasonable grounds for believing the truth of what they said, or was not negligent in other ways (such as in failing to answer a question), the insurer should have no remedy for misrepresentation or non-disclosure.

(3) If a consumer proposer has made a negligent misrepresentation, the court should apply a proportionate remedy by asking what the insurer would have done had it known the true facts. In particular:

  (a) Where an insurer would have excluded a particular type of claim, the insurer should not be obliged to pay claims that would fall within the exclusion;

  (b) Where an insurer would have declined the risk altogether, the claim may be refused;

  (c) Where an insurer would have charged more, the claim should be reduced proportionately to the under-payment of premium.

For business insurance, on point (c), we asked whether the remedy for negligent misrepresentation should be proportionate, in that it should aim to put the insurer into the position it would have been in had it known the true circumstances. "Basis of the contract" clauses, whether in the proposal form or the contract itself, should be ineffective to make all the answers given by the insured into warranties. (This was a provisional proposal to be discussed further in the current paper, and was without prejudice to the decision whether or not to permit specific warranties of existing fact contained within the contract.)

Consumers

Our tentative proposal was that in the consumer market, insurers should ask consumers clear questions about any matter that is material to them and that there should be no duty of disclosure on consumers.

It should not be possible to contract out of the new rules governing consumer insurance except in favour of the consumer.

Businesses

We tentatively proposed that:

(1) The duty of disclosure should continue to apply to business insurance contracts in general.

(2) The law affecting business insurance should be changed to give the insured certain additional rights, but that the rules should in general not be mandatory.

(3) We tentatively proposed that our earlier proposals for business insurance should apply to MAT; and we asked if there is any reason not to apply our earlier proposals for business insurance to reinsurance.

Small Businesses

We asked:

(1) To what extent small businesses should be treated in the same way as consumers.

(2) How small businesses should be defined for this purpose.

A change in approach: mandatory rules for business insurance

In the light of the discussion of these proposals at the seminars, we have revised our approach on the question whether, in the case of business insurance, it should be possible for the parties to agree to vary the rules in favour of the insurer. We had suggested that in business insurance this should be permissible, but it should not be possible to agree to a 'basis of the contract' clause.

In the seminar we were asked whether it was consistent to permit business parties to alter the rules on misrepresentation by agreement while at the same time forbidding them to use basis of the contract clauses. To some extent they are just different ways of reaching the same result; why forbid one but allow the other? The same question will arise in relation to warranties as to specific facts: why should the parties not be able to create specific warranties, so that they have remedies even for non-negligent misstatements, if they can achieve much the same result by altering the rules on misrepresentation? Shouldn't both sets of rules be mandatory?

We had thought not. We had thought that there is a difference between remedies for misrepresentation and remedies for breach of warranty that justified a difference in treatment. In the context of insurance contract law, the parties' freedom of contract should not be interfered with unless strictly necessary. However we need to ensure, so far as reasonably possible, that the parties understand the effect of what they are agreeing to. This is the problem with warranties of fact: as we pointed out earlier, the effects are most unlikely to accord with the reasonable expectations of the insured. We thought that an insured was much less likely to be taken by surprise by a clause dis-applying the normal rules governing misrepresentation in favour of the insurer.

We were thinking of a provision such as that "the insurer should have the right to avoid the contract even if the proposer's misstatement were made without negligence". That kind of provision should put the insured on warning. It makes it reasonably clear to the insured what its position will be if it makes an inaccurate or incomplete statement. Therefore we had in mind to allow the parties to alter the rules on misrepresentation but not to give effect to specific warranties of fact, even in business insurance.

However we have to admit that our argument is only a good one so far as insureds will in practice become aware of the clause. Moreover, it was rightly pointed out that the rules on misrepresentation could be excluded by a clause stating simply "section 000 of the Insurance Contract Act 2*xxx* shall not apply to this contract". Even if they read this clause, few non-expert insureds would be much the wiser.

We now think our approach was incorrect. We suspect that a contractual clause that alters the rules on avoidance for misrepresentation is less likely to put the insured on notice of the risk being placed on it than is a statement that it warrants the truth of specified facts. In other words, we think we were wrong to suggest that the rules on misrepresentation could be varied by agreement. If it is desired to allow insurers to reserve the right to refuse a claim because of a wholly innocent misstatement of existing fact, it is probably better to allow it to do so via a warranty of the truth of the facts than by a clause altering the remedies for misrepresentation.

We return to the question of warranties as to specific facts below. Meanwhile, we tentatively propose that, contrary to what we said in our first Issues Paper, the proposed rules on materiality and non-fraudulent misrepresentation should be mandatory in business and consumer insurance.

WARRANTIES OF PAST OR EXISTING FACT

Abolishing basis of the contract clauses

There are three main problems with basis of the contract clauses:

(1) The insurer is not required to distinguish between material and immaterial issues: instead, it can grant warranty status en bloc to all the answers in a proposal form, whether they are material or not.

(2) Such clauses allow insurers to apply a remedy appropriate to warranties to statements that are really representations. If the law of misrepresentation were to be reformed to reduce the remedies available to insurers for non-fraudulent misrepresentations, insurers could use basis of the contract clauses to evade the reforms. They could, for example, avoid liability for misrepresentations that are innocent and nonnegligent; for negligent misrepresentations, they could avoid all liability rather than applying a proportionate remedy.

(3) The warranty does not need to appear in the policy itself. Policyholders will rarely understand the import of what may seem to be obscure words at the bottom of a proposal form.

There are several approaches to removing these problems.

(1) The law could allow statements to be incorporated en bloc, but only if the incorporation clause were in the policy itself. This is the current law for marine insurance. Section 35(2) of the Marine Insurance Act 1906 states that the warranty must either be in the

policy, or "contained in some document incorporated by reference to the policy". This means that a policy may contain a clause that has the effect of converting all the statements in the proposal form into warranties. However, the incorporation clause must be in the policy itself. By contrast, in other types of insurance, the incorporation clause may be on the proposal form only.

(2) The legislation could permit an insurer to convert a statement of existing fact into a warranty, but only if it did so as a specific term of the policy. This was the approach taken by the Law Commission's 1980 report. It would allow a statement of existing fact to be treated as a warranty, but only if the statement itself were in the policy. It would prevent all statements on a proposal form from being incorporated as warranties en bloc.

(3) The legislation could state that all statements of existing fact made by the insured should be regarded as representations rather than warranties. Thus if the statement were inaccurate, the insurer's remedies would be those available for misrepresentation, not for breach of warranty. This means, for example, that an insurer could not avoid liability for an innocent misstatement, even if it was written into the contract. This is the approach taken by the Australian Insurance Contracts Act 1984, section 24. It provides that a statement by the insured about the existence of a current state of affairs should take effect only as a representation, not as a warranty.

The last option is the most radical, since it would mean that even specific warranties of existing fact would have no special status; they would merely be representations. This would be so whether they were warranties of specific facts or became warranties by virtue of a general "basis of the contract" clause. We consider this radical third option after discussing whether basis of the contract clauses should continue to be effective, without prejudice to the question of specific warranties. We consider consumer insurance first and then business insurance.

Basis of the Contract Clauses in Consumer Insurance

Even if warranties as to specific facts are still to be effective in business insurance, we are convinced that in consumer insurance, basis of the contract clauses should not be effective. We raised this question in our first Issues Paper on Misrepresentation and Non-disclosure, noting there has been widespread criticism of their use. In 1997, for example, the National Consumer Council described them as "completely unfair". Although the ICOB Rules do not refer to basis of the contract clauses, their use was barred by the 1986 SGIP. The ABI has told us that the use of such clauses contravenes insurers' duty to treat customers fairly. They have been outlawed in Australia and New Zealand. At the first working seminar there seemed to be widespread agreement with the suggestion in our Issues Paper that basis of the contract clauses should always be ineffective in consumer insurance.

In consumer insurance it would not be adequate to reform the law merely by requiring that the warranty must either be in the policy, or "contained in some document incorporated by reference to the policy". If all that is required were that there should be a clause in the policy that the insured warrants the truth of every statement made in another document, such as the proposal form, consumers would be no more likely to understand the effect than if the "basis of the contract" clause were in the proposal form. At the very least (and as will be seen in the next section, we would go further) we think that in consumer insurance warranties of existing fact should be effective only if each fact warranted is specifically set out in the policy or in a schedule to it.

We tentatively propose that "basis of the contract" and similar clauses that have the effect of turning statements of fact in general into warranties should be of no effect in consumer contracts. "Basis of the contract" clauses in business insurance

Here we consider whether, if warranties as to facts are to remain effective, they should have to be created by the policy itself, rather than through a basis of the contract clause on a proposal form. Later we discuss whether to take a more radical approach, to say that all statements of existing fact made by the insured should be regarded as representations rather than warranties.

In the Issues Paper on Misrepresentation and Non-disclosure we tentatively proposed that basis of the contract clauses should no longer be effective in business insurance. There would need at least to be a provision that incorrect answers would not give rise to a remedy for breach of warranty unless there was a term to that effect in the contract itself, rather than merely a "basis of the contract" clause in the proposal form. In effect, if a statement made by the insured were to amount to a warranty it would have to be stated in the policy or in a document incorporated by reference. This is a rule that would have to be mandatory, otherwise the mere insertion of a "basis of the contract" clause might be taken as a 'contracting out' from all the rules proposed in this section.

Again at the working seminar there seemed to be wide support for this, which is already the position in marine insurance. The only query raised was whether it was consistent to make this a mandatory rule while we had suggested that in business insurance it should be possible to contract out of the proposed restrictions on avoidance for misrepresentation. We discussed this question above. In any event, the thrust of the argument seemed to be that both sets of rules should be mandatory, so it does not affect the present discussion.

As will be seen below, we would consider going further than denying effect to basis of the contract clauses in business insurance; we ask whether all statements of existing fact made by the insured should be regarded as representations rather than warranties, as in the next section we will propose for consumer insurance.

However, as a minimum, we tentatively propose that in business insurance, a "basis of the contract" clause in the proposal form should no longer be effective to turn the statements made by the proposer into warranties. Each statement of fact warranted should be set out either in the policy, or in some document incorporated by reference to the policy. This rule would be mandatory. Specific warranties as to past or existing fact

Consumer Insurance

In our first Issues Paper on the law of misrepresentation and non-disclosure, we suggested that the remedies proposed for misrepresentation should be mandatory in consumer insurance contracts, but default rules in business insurance contracts. In other words, for consumer insurance, an insurer's remedies for a mis-statement of fact should be those set out in the new legislation: an insurer would not be entitled to add to those remedies by a term in the contract.

It would be consistent with this still to permit the insurer to rely on specific warranties of fact that were set out in a written document (or some similar formal requirement). This appears to have been the view of the Law Commission in 1980. The report recommended that basis of the contract clauses should be of no effect but specific warranties as to past or existing fact would be effective, subject to two provisos:

(1) The warranty must be material (there would be a presumption that it was material); and

(2) Once a claim had occurred, the insurer would not be entitled to refuse to pay the claim if the insured showed that the warranty was not intended to safeguard against the kind of event that materialised or that the breach of warranty did not increase the risk of the event occurring in the way it did.

The requirements of materiality and of some connection between the warranty and the claim would limit the possibility for the insurer to use specific warranties as a way to avoid any restrictions on the current remedies for misrepresentation. Suppose, for example, that an insurance policy contained the following term: The insured hereby warrants that the house in question is made of brick and slate.

If the house was in fact timber-framed under a brick skin, the insurer would be able to serve notice on the insured repudiating the contract from the date of the notice if no claim had yet arisen; but if an event giving rise to a claim had occurred, whether the insurer would have to meet the claim would depend on the facts. If the event were a flood, the insurer would have to pay. If the event were a fire, it would depend on whether the construction of the house had increased the risk of the event that occurred. So a claim for smoke damage caused by a chippan fire might have to be met whereas a fire that affected the main structure might be different.

We now think this "specific warranty" approach would offer insufficient protection to consumers. First, it would still provide the insurer with the right to refuse a claim even though the consumer had not been fraudulent or even negligent. Secondly, we doubt that consumers would derive much protection from the formal requirements. Merely requiring that the warranty is put into a written document which is given to the consumer within a reasonable time will only protect the consumer who reads the document. Even if the statements have to be in a separate document from the body of the policy, we doubt that many consumers will read them. Normally they will only receive the document after they have, in their view, completed arranging their insurance.

This suggests that we should take the wide approach of the Australian Insurance Contracts Act 1984, namely that a statement of existing fact cannot be a warranty. The insurer's remedies should be those available for misrepresentation (which would not permit avoidance for an innocent, non-negligent misrepresentation, and would apply a proportionate remedy to a negligent one). If the clause were treated as a warranty it would allow an insurer to evade the reforms by applying a different (more insurer-friendly) set of remedies to any breach.

It might be objected that this restriction would be easy to evade. It would be open to the insurer to define the cover by stating that the insurance only applied to houses constructed of brick and slate. In consumer cases, we think current law provides adequate safeguards through the Unfair Terms in Consumer Contract Regulations 1999. The effect of these was explained in detail in Part 4. In the example above, if the restriction to brick houses was explained upfront and in a clear and transparent way, the term would be classified as a core term and would not be open to review. If the exclusion was only mentioned in the small print, it would be subject to a fairness test. We think that is a just result. A consumer who is told that the insurance offered applies only to certain types of risk and not others, or who is given documents that make this quite clear without the consumer having to read the small print, does not have legitimate grounds for complaint. With warranties of fact the situation is different. The reason for limiting the use of warranties as to existing facts is precisely because consumers are very unlikely to understand the effect of the warranty.

We tentatively propose that in consumer insurance, all statements of existing fact should be treated as representations rather than warranties.

SHOULD SPECIFIC WARRANTIES OF FACT BE EFFECTIVE?

We have already proposed, as we did in our first Issues Paper, that in business insurance basis of the contract clauses should not be effective to make every statement in the proposal form into a warranty and thus give the insurer the right to repudiate. The reason for this is that to allow basis of the contract clauses would permit the insurer in effect to exclude the regime we proposed for misrepresentation by means of a single clause,10 which most business insureds would not understand. This rule should be mandatory.

As we said in the case of consumer insurance, it would be consistent with rendering basis of the contract clauses ineffective still to permit the insurer to rely on specific warranties of fact that were set out in a written document (or some similar formal requirement). The question is whether this should also be prevented, as we have tentatively proposed for consumer insurance, or whether it should be permitted, either as at present or subject to restrictions.

There are two reasons why an insurer might want to turn a statement of fact into a warranty rather than rely on the remedies we have suggested for misrepresentation:

(1) It does not have to show that the statement was material.

(2) It will be discharged whether or not the insured was in any way at fault.

In neither case, under current law, does there have to be any connection between the incorrect statement and the loss for which the claim is made.

As to the causal connection, we explain below that we think a causal connection of the kind envisaged by the 1980 report should be required for warranties as to the future. A principal reason is that the insured will normally assume that it is still covered for risks that have nothing to do with the warranty. We see no reason to adopt a different approach with warranties as to existing fact. Again the insured is likely to assume that only risks to which the warranty is relevant will be affected.

However the law on misrepresentation would not be changed in this respect. Unless the statement was immaterial or the insured otherwise acted reasonably, the insurer will be entitled to a remedy without having to show that the misstatement and the claim were linked. Thus in this respect the insurer's remedies for misrepresentation would be less restricted than those proposed for breach of warranty.

As to materiality, we saw that the 1980 report would have limited the insurer's rights where the matter warranted was not material. We too see no reason why an insurer should be entitled to remedies for something that a reasonable insured would think irrelevant, even if it is written into the contract.

Again the insured may simply (and reasonably) not realise what is wanted. However we quite agree with the 1980 report's recommendation that a statement incorporated as a warranty should be presumed to be material unless the insured shows otherwise. In any event, it should not be difficult for the insurer to make it clear to the insured what facts are material to the insurer.

The principal question arises where the insured was not at fault. Do insurers need the right to turn a statement of fact into a warranty so that they will have a right to refuse to pay the claim, or treat the policy as discharged, even though the proposer's misrepresentation was innocent and not negligent?

We do not see that they do. As we argued in our first Issues Paper, the risk of non-negligent misrepresentations is one that should normally be pooled. Therefore we think that the "default" position, at least, should be that if the untrue statement was made without fraud or negligence, the insurer should have no remedy whether for misrepresentation or breach of warranty.

SHOULD THE RULES BE MANDATORY?

That leaves a difficult question: should the parties be free to agree that the insurer should have the right to refuse to pay a claim or (to use neutral language) to end the policy because of an incorrect statement made without either fraud or negligence?

In our first Issues Paper we had proposed that, in business insurance, the insurer should be able to give itself the right to avoid for negligent or even wholly innocent misrepresentations, as in business insurance the new rules on misrepresentation would not be mandatory. As we explained earlier, we now think this was the wrong approach. If the insurer should be allowed to give itself remedies for "non-negligent" misstatements, the permitted way of doing this should be by the insured giving warranties of specific facts.

Were the law to be changed so as to prevent the insurer being able to rely on warranties as to specific facts (as in Australian law), that rule itself should be mandatory. To make it merely a default rule that could be altered by agreement would render it ineffective. Insurers could simply insert into their contracts a clause disapplying the relevant section of the new legislation and then continue to use specific warranties.

Indeed the court might find that the parties had implicitly excluded the new rule simply because there is a warranty of fact in the contract. In either case, the insured who is not an expert will still not be aware of the potential consequences. In other words, any new "no warranties of fact" rule would have to be mandatory to have any effect at all.

So a choice has to be made. The alternatives are:

(1) To continue to allow breach of warranties of specific facts to act as a defence to a claim provided the claim was causally connected with the breach. We think that specific warranties should be permitted only subject to formal safeguards, such as that the warranty is in a separate written schedule to the policy. We also think that an insurer should only be entitled to reject a claim on the ground of breach of warranty if there was a causal connection between the breach and the claim. We discuss these points in more detail in relation to warranties as to the future; or

(2) To provide both that the insurer's remedy for a misstatement of fact should only be through the remedies for misrepresentation, and that the rules governing these should be mandatory. This is the position in Australian law.

This choice is difficult and we would welcome views.

In Business Insurance, we Invite Views on Whether:

(1) incorrect statements of past or existing fact should only amount to misrepresentations and not warranties (which would be a mandatory rule); or

(2) breach of warranty of specific facts should continue to act as a defence to a claim provided the claim was causally connected with the breach, and that certain formal safeguards as to warranties generally had been satisfied when the contract was made.

Other types of clause dealing with existing facts.

That leaves a question about policies that seek to achieve the same result by employing a narrow definition of the risk to be covered or an exception to the risk, for example by excluding from cover houses that are not built of brick and slate. The same issue arises in relation to warranties as to the future and is discussed below.

WARRANTIES AS TO THE FUTURE: A WRITTEN STATEMENT

In 1980, the Law Commission recommended that insurers should not be entitled to rely on a breach of warranty unless the insured was supplied with a written statement of the warranty either at or before the contract was made, or as soon as possible thereafter. This recommendation is particularly relevant to promissory warranties, whereby the insured "undertakes that some particular thing shall or shall not be done". However it would have applied also to the specific warranties as to past or existing fact that the Law Commission then thought should be permitted.

The law already requires that in marine policies express warranties must be in writing. We think that this requirement should extend to all forms of insurance. Where cover is conditional on an insured carrying out a specific task, or refraining from an activity that would be normal in the circumstances, it is important that there should be clarity on both sides about what is required. We think the insured's obligations should be set out in writing and included or referred to in the main contract document. For these purposes, writing would include printed and electronic forms.

We tentatively propose that a claim should only be refused because the insured has failed to comply with a contractual obligation, if the obligation is set out in writing and included or referred to in the main contract document.

For consumer insurance, it should not be enough for the warranty to be buried somewhere in the small print of an insurance policy. The insurer should take specific steps to bring the obligation to the insured's attention. This is already regarded as good practice: ICOB Rule 5 requires that significant or unusual terms are brought to a consumer's attention. And, as we discussed in Appendix B, the FOS already makes enforcement of the term dependent on this requirement. We found several cases where the FOS refused to uphold an unusual term if it was not brought to the customer's attention.

We think the same protections should apply in a court of law. Like the FOS, a court should only enforce a specific obligation on the consumer if the insurer took sufficient steps to bring it to the consumer's attention. The insurer should spell out both what the consumer must do (as in "you must fit a five-lever mortice lock") and the consequences of not doing so (as in "if you do not, we may refuse any claim connected with your failure").

There are different approaches to implementing this principle. One would be to impose detailed rules about how policyholders' obligations should be spelled out. For example, rules could state that the obligation should be in the product summary (required by ICOB Rule 5.3.1); or on the cover note; or in a separate letter; on in one of the three. The statement could be required to be in plain language, legible and clearly presented; or one could go further and specify a minimum point size and prescribed warning. The FSA already has powers to make rules of this sort.

The alternative would be to set out the general principle that unusual terms should be brought to the consumers' attention. It would then be left to the courts to decide whether the obligation has been complied with, bearing in mind any relevant FSA rules or guidance.

The first approach is more certain; the second is more flexible. It is more adaptable to new methods of sales and product information. Given the FSA's current emphasis towards a more principles-based approach, with fewer detailed rules, we are inclined to favour the second approach. This would mean that a court would be left to decide whether the insurer had met its obligation to bring the warranty or similar obligation to the policyholder's attention, having regard to any rules or guidance specified by the FSA.

In consumer insurance, we tentatively propose that an insurer may only refuse a claim on the grounds that the insured has failed to carry out a specific task (or refrained from a normal activity) if it has taken sufficient steps to bring the requirement to the insured's attention. In deciding whether the insurer has taken sufficient steps, the court should have regard to FSA rules or guidance.

REQUIRING A CONNECTION BETWEEN THE BREACH AND THE LOSS

The greatest and most obvious problem with the law on warranties is that it permits the insurer to escape liability for technical breaches that have nothing to do with the loss in question.

We think there is a need to introduce some form of causal connection test to protect policyholders from unfair treatment. An insured may readily agree to a warranty that their sprinkler system will be inspected, believing that if the failure of the sprinkler system causes a loss they will not be indemnified. However, policyholders would not understand this to mean that the insurers would refuse to pay if the breach were later remedied, or if the loss were totally unconnected with the sprinklers. This result defies logic and normal expectations, is inconsistent with good practice as recognised by the SGIP and risks bringing the UK insurance industry into disrepute. Whether we are discussing consumer or business insurance, the current law can properly be described as unjust.

We tentatively conclude that the law should afford policyholders some protection against claims being denied for reasons unconnected with the loss.

Although our general policy is clear, difficult questions arise about how this policy should be implemented. There are several possible models to follow. Both New Zealand and Australia have enacted statutes requiring some form of connection. Similarly, in 1980 the Law Commission proposed that an insured should be able to challenge the insurer's decision not to pay a claim if there were shown to be no links between the breach and the loss. Their recommendations were explained earlier.

There are similarities in these three models. For example, all three put the burden of proof firmly on the insured to show a lack of connection. However, the provisions differ in the words they use to define the type of causal connection required. There are also differences in scope: the 1980 report applied just to warranties, while the New Zealand legislation, for example, applied to any term which limited liability for events or circumstances likely to increase the risk of a loss.

Here we look first at how to define the causal connection required, and then at the scope of any reform.

Defining the Causal Connection

The three provisions use different words to describe the connection required between the breach and the loss. The Bill in the Law Commission's 1980 Report required the insured to prove that the breach did not "*increase the risk*" that the event giving rise to the claim would occur in the way it did. Under the New Zealand Act, the insured must prove that the event did not "*cause or contribute to*" the loss. In Australia the insured need only prove that it did not "*cause*" the loss.

We have considered whether there is any substantive difference between "increasing the risk" of a loss, "contributing to" a loss or "causing" a loss. The Australian Law Reform Commission thought there was, and criticised the English wording as being too narrow.

The ALRC pointed out that even if a breach did not cause or contribute to the loss, it might increase the risk that the loss would occur. It mentioned the example of modifications to a car that increased the risk that the brakes would fail. The ALRC suggested that if a collision was caused entirely by the driver's carelessness, and the brakes worked admirably, the modifications might still be said to have increased the risk of a collision. It thought that in such a case the insurer should have to pay, and so it recommended the insured need only prove that the breach did not "*cause*" the loss.

This result does not necessarily follow from the words used. A court could decide that "the way the accident did in fact occur" was that brakes worked perfectly. Therefore, the modifications did not "increase the risk" of this particular accident. However, examples given in the 1980 report suggest that the Law Commission did intend a restrictive approach. One example was a fidelity policy where the insured employer promised not to employ staff without first taking up satisfactory references. The Law Commission stated that if an employer failed to take up references on an employee, who then stole the employer's money, the insurer should "clearly be entitled to reject the claim, because the commercial purpose of the warranty was to guard against this very type of loss". It "should not be open to the insured to resist this by seeking to show, for instance, that A would have produced satisfactory or forged references if he had been asked for any". Thus the Law Commission did not envisage that the insured would bring evidence of whether the breach affected this particular loss in these circumstances.

By contrast, the Australian approach appears more generous to policyholders. The insured need only show that the insured's act or omission did not "cause" a claim. This might suggest that the breach must be a dominant or major cause of the loss, or that the loss would not have happened but for the breach. For example, car insurance might include a warranty that the car should not be driven by someone under 25. Suppose that while the car was being driven by a 20 year old, it was involved in an accident caused primarily by the negligence of an uninsured cyclist. It is generally accepted that the youth of a driver increases the risk of an accident. However, in these particular circumstances it could be argued that the driver's age did not "cause" the accident. Yet it might still seem fair to reject the claim. Unless there is strong evidence to the contrary, the fact that the driver was young and inexperienced would be a background factor contributing to the accident. Even if the cyclist was at fault, a more experienced driver might still have avoided a collision. The driver's age might therefore be said to increase the risk of a loss or to contribute to the loss.

Our Provisional View

In our view, the onus should be on the insured to show that the breach did not contribute in any way to the accident. This means that in the modified car, the insured would be able to show that in fact the modifications did not "contribute" to the accident by proving that the brakes worked perfectly or that the car's braking capacity was completely irrelevant to the accident. It would also be open to the insured to attempt to prove that the failure to take up references did not contribute to the loss because the employee's references would have been satisfactory.

However, the insured would need to prove this on the balance of probabilities. It would not be sufficient simply to invite the court to speculate about "might have beens". Normally, a failure to follow proper procedures would contribute towards an employee theft. Similarly, the age and inexperience of a driver would be expected to contribute to an accident, even a no-fault accident. The insured would have to do more than merely show that the breach was not the main or dominant cause of the loss.

We tentatively propose that the policyholder should be entitled to be paid a claim if it can prove on the balance of probability that the event or circumstances constituting the breach of warranty did not contribute to the loss.

Payment of Premium Warranties

At present, insurers may include "payment of premium warranties", under which the insured warrants that premium instalments will be paid within specific time limits. In *JA Chapman v Kadirga and others*, it was held that if such a warranty was breached, the insurer is automatically discharged from any further liability under the contract, but the insured remains liable to pay all the premiums on the due date. This appears to be a harsh result.

Late payment of a premium will almost never cause or contribute to a loss. It is therefore worth considering what effect a payment of premium warranty would have under our reforms. It would still be open to an insurer to make payment by the due date into a condition of the policy. Under normal contractual principles, if the insured breached the condition, this would be considered a repudiatory breach. It would be open to the insured to accept the repudiation and terminate the contract. Until a repudiatory breach is accepted, the contract continues and any claim must be paid. Once accepted, both parties' obligations come to an end, so that an insured would not be liable for any payments arising after the termination (though the insured may be liable to pay damages for the insurer's loss of profits). We think this is a fairer approach, and consider it in more detail below.

Partial Loss

The Australian provisions protect policyholders when a breach of warranty causes only part of the loss. Section 54(4) of the Australian Insurance Contracts Act 1984 states that: Where the insured proves that some part of the loss that gave rise to the claim was not caused by the act, the insurer may not refuse to pay the claim, so far as it concerns that part of the loss, by reason only of the act. For example, if a fire spreads from a well-maintained section of a building (A) to one where the sprinklers are not working (B), the insured is entitled to the part of their claim relating to the well-maintained section.

On balance, we think that such a provision is fair to policyholders, and a useful clarification of the causal connection test. If the fire spreads from section A to section B, the faults in section B cannot be said to have contributed to the loss in section A. It would, of course be different if the fire spreads from the faulty section. Here the breach would have contributed to the further loss. We welcome views.

We tentatively propose that the law should provide that if a breach contributes to only part of a loss, the insurer may not refuse to pay the part not related to the breach.

A Mandatory or Default Rule?

We have said that the current rule is unjust because it defeats the reasonable expectations of the insured. We think this will almost always be the case in consumer insurance, and we recommend that for consumers the rule should be mandatory. For business insurance it is perhaps arguable that it should be possible to alter the rule provided very clear words are used to do so.

We tentatively propose that the causal connection rule should be mandatory in consumer insurance. We invite views on whether it should also be mandatory in business insurance.

OTHER TYPES OF CLAUSE

The 1980 Report applied only to warranties. For example, if the insured "warranted to maintain the car in a roadworthy condition", then it would be open to the insured to argue that a fault with the headlights could not have increased the risk of a loss in broad daylight.

However, if the same provision were expressed as a description of the risk (that the insurance only applied while the car was roadworthy) then the insured could not take advantage of the defence, and the insurer would not be required to pay the claim.

We think it would be unduly formalistic to confine the causal connection test to warranties. Birds and Hird are right to argue that this would merely encourage insurers to find other means of achieving the same ends.

Both the New Zealand and Australian legislation take a more purposive approach. For example, the New Zealand 1977 Act applies to a provision in an insurance contract that meets two tests.

(1) They must "exclude or limit the liability of the insurer... on the happening of certain events or the existence of certain circumstances"; and

(2) this must be because the events or circumstances were (in the view of the insurer) "likely to increase the risk of such loss occurring".

A provision stating that the car was only insured while it was roadworthy would be caught by the section. This clause purports to exclude or limit the liability of the insurer in certain circumstances (that the car is unroadworthy) because when a car is unroadworthy, the risk of a loss increases. In contrast, the reform would not affect a notice clause. A failure to give notice could not increase the risk of a loss occurring as it would only apply once a loss had happened. Similarly, it would not affect a payment provision, as a failure to pay a premium does not increase the risk of a loss.

Our Provisional View

Our tentative proposal is that the reforms should follow the New Zealand approach: they should extend beyond warranties, to all terms that enable the insurer to refuse to pay a claim for events or circumstances that add to the risk of loss. It should not matter whether a clause is written as a warranty ("the insured warrants that the vehicle will be maintained in a roadworthy condition") or as descriptive of the risk ("the insurance only applies if the vehicle is in a roadworthy condition"). In either case, the insurer should not be entitled to refuse a claim for a fault that has no connection to the loss: for example, a fault with the headlamps should not affect an accident in daylight. If the reform were confined to warranties, it would simply encourage insurers to draft policies in more ingenious ways.

Should the protection apply to any term that purports to exclude or limit the liability of the insurer for events or circumstances that are thought to increase the risk of a loss occurring?

A Proviso: where an Activity is wholly Outside the Policy

That said, we have a particular concern where the insured has taken out a policy that is meant to be used for one purpose, activity or place and is trying to use the insurance for an entirely different purpose, activity or place.

The obvious example from the case law is where an insured has taken out a motor policy for a private car, and is using it for commercial purposes. If the insured has used the car for one business trip, the law should not invalidate the whole policy. However, if the car is being used full time as a taxi there comes a point where the activity generating the loss is so far removed from the activity covered by the policy that the policy should not apply at all. If the car is stolen when parked overnight in the insured's driveway, it is arguable that the insurer should not be liable for the claim even if the insured could prove that the theft was not related to its use as a taxi.

Another example would be third party, fire and theft car insurance limited to owners aged over 30. Suppose the car was owned and driven by a 20 year old at all times. Under the Road Traffic Act the insurers would be required to meet third party claims. We are not sure that the insured should be able to demand that a theft claim was also paid because the age of the driver did not contribute to the theft. Again there comes a point in which the purpose to which the loss relates is so far removed from the purpose covered by the policy that the claim is not within the terms of the policy at all.

A similar example from marine insurance would be an exclusion for a war risk area, such as the Gulf. If a ship enters the Gulf, this should not automatically discharge the insurer from liability. Instead, when the ship leaves the Gulf, cover should resume. However, if the ship is in the Gulf at the time of a loss, it is arguable that no claim should be paid, even if the loss was not related to a war risk and could have happened anywhere.

We think that the causal connection should not apply where the insurance relates to one purpose, activity or place, and the loss arises from an entirely different purpose or activity or in another place. In deciding whether the purpose, activity or place is entirely different, the court should ask whether the difference was such that a reasonable insured could have expected the loss to be covered. Thus we do not think that a 20 year old owner could reasonably expect to be covered by a policy limited to those over 30; nor would a reasonable ship owner expect to be covered in an excluded war risk zone. However, a car owner would expect to be covered for a car with broken headlamps that was driven during the day.

The court should also differentiate between occasional misuse and constant misuse. For example, if a car covered by private insurance were used occasionally for a business purpose, this would suspend cover for accidents related to the business use, but would not affect unconnected claims. However, if the car were always used for business purposes, this would take it outside the terms of the policy altogether.

We think the way to build in a limitation of this kind would be to use a test of what it was reasonable for the insured to expect. This would vary according to the facts and the nature of the insurance. Should the causal connection test be subject to an exception where the insurance relates to one purpose, activity or place, and the loss arises from another purpose or activity or in another place? In these circumstances the claim should not be paid if the loss related to an activity which was so far outside the terms of the cover that a reasonable insured could not have expected the loss to be covered.

An Alternative Approach

We accept that requiring a causal link subject to a proviso adds a measure of complexity to the law. An alternative way of dealing with the same problem would be to take an "unfair terms approach". This would ask whether the term that entitled the insurer to avoid liability met a requirement of fairness. We consider this approach in more detail in Part 8. The advantage of applying a fairness test to cases such as these is that it is more flexible. It looks at the heart of the matter – was the term fair in all the circumstances, taking into account what was reasonably expected, what the insured understood by it, and the legitimate interests of the insurer? The disadvantage is that a fairness test is more uncertain. The need to look at all the circumstances encourages greater litigation.

SHOULD THE REFORMS APPLY TO MARINE, AVIATION AND TRANSPORT INSURANCE?

In 1980, the Law Commission excluded Marine, Aviation and Transport (MAT) insurance from the scope of its reforms. It argued that the people working in this market were generally professionals "who could reasonably be expected to be aware of the niceties of insurance law".25 The law was certain and understood, and worked satisfactorily.

In our first paper on non-disclosure and misrepresentation we argued against making a distinction between MAT and other forms of insurance. We were not convinced that MAT was a separate and distinct market.26 We thought it would be overly complex to require lawyers to apply one law to (for example) major constructions, and quite a different law to ships.

That said, there are reasons why marine warranties may need to be considered separately from warranties in other contracts. First, the English courts have tended to construe warranties more strictly in marine cases than in other forms of insurance. Secondly, the MIA 1906 implies warranties into marine insurance contracts by operation of law. The voyage conditions may also require review. Below we start by considering whether there are any good reasons for continuing to take a particularly strict approach to marine warranties. We then look specifically at the warranties implied into the marine insurance contracts by the MIA 1906 to see if a causal connection test should be applied to them. Finally, we ask whether we should review those voyage conditions within the MIA that discharge insurers from liability for reasons unconnected with the risk.

The Arguments for Strict Construction

The doctrine that marine warranties should be strictly construed has a long history. Developed by Lord Mansfield in the Eighteenth Century,27 it was enshrined in the 1906 Act and upheld by the House of Lords in *The Good Luck* as recently as 1992. Lord Goff justified the doctrine in the following terms: The rationale of warranties in insurance law is that the insurer only accepts the risk provided that the warranty is fulfilled. This is entirely understandable; and it follows that the immediate effect of a breach of a promissory warranty is to discharge the insurer from liability as from the date of the breach.

The difficulty, however, is that the breach is usually only discovered after a loss has occurred. Where the loss is related to the breach, the doctrine is clearly understandable. But where the breach relates to a different risk, and no loss has materialised from that particular breach, the remedy can seem arbitrary and excessive.

We can understand that a strict approach had some justification when the doctrine was developed. In 1786, insurers had almost no information about the ship or the risk, except for what the insured told them and what the insured promised he would do. If the insured promised to do something, and then did not do it, it undermined his credibility and therefore the whole nature of the risk. However, the amount of information available to insurers has changed beyond recognition.

The ISM and ISPS Codes, for example, require a large body of records to be kept, including records of training, shipboard operations, security threats, potential hazards, internal audits and reviews. This means that marine risks are much more like other risks in the market. Insurers are less dependent on the good faith of the insured, but can verify the information given through a variety of surveys and audits. It also means that they are more aware of technical breaches, even if those breaches did not result in any loss.

It has been put to us that a breach of warranty continues to undermine the credibility of the insured, and hence the nature of the risk, even in the absence of any specific causal connection between the two. In the *Bamcell II*, for example, the policyholders had specifically promised to place a watchman on board each night from 2200 hours to 0600 hours, but in fact had never hired a watchman at all. It could be argued that such behaviour fundamentally altered the nature of the risk. If the insured could not be trusted to do as they had promised, how many other unacceptable risks were they taking? Even without a direct causal connection between the lack of a watchman and the daytime loss, could there be said to be a connection through the addition of a moral hazard?

We have two concerns about this argument. The first is that behaviour that seems heinous to an insurer may seem innocuous to an outsider. There are several examples in the law reports, where (for example) insurers have argued that a minor conviction many years ago fundamentally alters the nature of the risk, in ways that the court has been unable to accept.29 The doctrine of warranties allows the insurer to play judge and jury by denying a claim when they think that the insured has committed a morally reprehensible breach, even for matters that appear merely technical to others.

Secondly, we do not think that the present rules on warranties meet the needs and expectations of an international market. We have not found any commentators outside the common law sphere who consider it is fair for an insurer to fail to pay a claim for a breach which is not connected to the loss. Several criticise the rule in scathing terms.30 Even within jurisdictions that share the legacy of the Marine Insurance Act, it is rare for a court to accept insurers' arguments that a claim unrelated to a breach should not be paid. It was rejected by the US Supreme Court in *Wilburn Boat*, and by the Supreme Court of Canada in *Bamcell II*.31 The Australia Law Reform Commission reviewed marine insurance law in 2001, following complaints from the fishing industry and recommended that a breach of warranty should only justify avoiding a claim if it proximately caused the loss.

Given the international nature of the marine market, it is particularly important that its legal rules should correspond to internationally accepted notions of fairness. For this reason, we tentatively propose that the causal connection test outlined above should also apply to marine insurance. The implied marine warranties

A full review of the implied warranties is outside the scope of our project. In 1980 we commented that the rules were long-established and well-known, and that the professionals in the market could reasonably be expected to be aware of their niceties.32 The rules are certainly well-established. How far they are well-known is difficult to say; even the short description in Appendix A reveals some complexities and uncertainties surrounding them. However, we have not received demands for their reform, and a full-scale review would take more resources than we have available.

Here we are concerned with only one limited question, which is whether the requirement for a causal connection set out above should also apply to the implied marine warranties. Our view is that it should. Below we consider the four warranties, to see if they raise any special issues.

Seaworthiness

The main effect would be upon the warranty of seaworthiness in voyage policies. It would effectively reverse the ruling in *De Hahn v Hartley*,33 by permitting warranties to be remedied. If, for example, a ship leaves port with insufficient crew, and later takes more crew on board, the insurer would be liable for subsequent losses. It would also mean that a technical breach (such as not carrying the required medicines, or not having the correct certificates on board) would not discharge the insurer from liability for an unconnected loss.

Our proposals are mild: in a voyage policy, the insured would only be paid if it could show, on the balance of probabilities that the breach did not contribute to the loss. This goes nowhere near as far as the requirement in time policies, where the *insurer* has to prove that the breach was a *real or dominant cause* of the loss. It does, however, go some way to lessening the difference between voyage and time policies. Given that the industry has lived with the time policy rule for over 100 years, we do not think that this lesser rule in voyage policies should cause undue difficulties.

Portworthiness and Cargoworthiness

These warranties are less likely to be a major cause of dispute, and we do not think that the proposed reform would have any great effect on the market.

At present, it may be possible for an insurer to argue that, if a problem in port is remedied before the ship is put to sea, the insurer is discharged from liability for an unconnected loss at sea. We do not think this result would be fair. Again, we believe that the insured should be able to put forward a defence that the breach did not contribute to the loss.

Legality

The warranty of legality raises more complex issues. Insurance contracts, like all other contracts are subject to the general doctrine of illegality. This means that if the parties agree to insure an illegal adventure, the contract would not be enforceable in any event. Similarly if, unbeknown to the insurer, the insured intended to engage in an illegal activity the contract would be unenforceable by the insured. These results are independent of the law on warranties, and would not be affected by the proposed reforms. The insured would not be entitled to enforce an illegal contract even if the loss was unconnected to the risks posed by the illegal conduct.

There is some uncertainty about how far the implied warranty of legality under section 41 of the MIA imposes additional requirements on insurance contracts. Under normal contract law, if one party commits a statutory offence in the course of performance (such as overloading a ship) this does not affect the enforceability of the contract.35 It is possible that section 41 goes further than normal contract law in these circumstances. If an insured could prevent the ship from being overloaded and fails to do so, this may be a breach of the implied warranty that "the adventure shall be carried out in a lawful manner". If this is a correct interpretation of the law, we think the rule needs to be tempered. Under our proposed reform, it would be open to the insured to argue that the overloading was not intended at the outset, but was only a subsequent illegality. If the insured could prove that the overloading did not contribute to the loss, the insurer would remain liable.

Overall, we see no reason why our causal connection test should not apply equally to implied and express warranties.

Is it agreed that the implied marine warranties should be subject to the same causal connection test as express warranties? Implied conditions as to the voyage

It is has been brought to our attention that there are other provisions within the Marine Insurance Act 1906 that operate in a similar way to warranties. For example, section 43 states that

Where the place of departure is specified in the policy, and the ship instead of sailing from that place sails from any other place, the risk does not attach.

This can lead to very technical arguments. For example, in *Molinos Nacionales v Pohjola Insurance Company Ltd*,36 the ship was said to sail from Tallinn, but instead sailed from Muuga, an adjacent part separated from Tallinn by a headland only 3 miles across, and managed by the same port authority. The difference in port had no bearing on the risk. Mr Justice Coleman described the insurer's argument that the risk did not attach as having "no merit whatsoever". However, the Act and earlier authorities permitted insurers to avoid a voyage policy for "trivial, entirely immaterial, deviations". He was therefore forced to conclude that the insurers should be allowed to defend the claim on these grounds, and were entitled to proceed to trial.

Other parts of the MIA raise similar issues. Under section 44, for example, the policy does not attach if the ship sails to the wrong destination. Under sections 45 and 46, if the destination is changed or there is a deviation, the insurer is discharged.

We intend to consult briefly about these sections at a later date.

SHOULD THE REFORMS APPLY TO REINSURANCE?

Our view is that unless there are very good reasons to the contrary, the law on reinsurance should follow, as closely as possible, the law that governs the original insurance contract.

An example of the problems that can be caused where the laws differ can be found in *Forsikringsaktieselkapet Vesta v Butcher*. The plaintiffs were a Norwegian insurance company who had insured the owners of a Norwegian fish farm against the loss of their fish. The plaintiffs had then reinsured 90% of the risk with London underwriters. Both the original policy and the reinsurance policy stated that a 24-hour watch be kept of the farm, and that "failure to comply" would render the policy null and void. Although the terms were identical, the applicable law was not. The original policy was governed by Norwegian law while the reinsurance policy was governed by English law.

The fish were lost in a storm. The farm had failed to keep a 24 hour watch, but this was unconnected to damage caused by the storm. Under Norwegian law, the breach did not prevent liability from arising, despite the express words of the policy, because it was not causative of the loss. The Norwegian insurers paid the claim.

However, when they sought to recover 90% of the loss from the London underwriters, the reinsurers pleaded breach of warranty. The House of Lords eventually held the reinsurers liable as, on a true construction of this particular policy, they had agreed to cover all the risks involved in the original policy. It was unfortunate, however, that the dispute took so long to resolve.

In 1980 the Law Commission recommended against extending the reforms to reinsurance contracts generally. It thought that the parties to reinsurance contracts would be "aware of the well-known and long-standing rules of law and practice governing the market in which they operate" and that its general recommendations on breach of warranty would be inappropriate to the market. It did however, attempt to protect insurers against the sort of anomalies that arose in the *Vesta* case. It recommended that where the reassured "substantially repeats the warranty broken by the insured", the reinsurer would not have greater rights against the reassured than the reassured had against the original policyholder.

We are not convinced that the parties to reinsurance are always fully aware of the differences between legal regimes. If they were, the difficulties in *Vesta* would not have arisen. The greater the variation in the law applying to different types of insurance contracts, the more scope there is for confusion to arise. We would not wish to create differences between insurance and reinsurance law unless those differences were clearly necessary. We fear that the specific provisions to prevent anomalies of the type suggested by the 1980 report would add to the complexity of the law.

We are interested to hear from the industry whether there are any reasons to treat reinsurance contracts differently. Our current thinking is that the reforms suggested above should apply to both insurance and reinsurance contracts.

Are there any reasons why the reforms should not apply to reinsurance contracts?

REFORMING OTHER PROVISIONS OF THE MIA 1906

The reforms we have tentatively proposed have consequences for the Marine Insurance Act 1906. For example, the requirement for a causal connection is incompatible with section 34(2), which does not allow a breach of warranty to be remedied before a loss occurs. Here we consider other implications of our proposals on reforming the MIA provisions on warranties. Automatic discharge or repudiation?

The reforms we have proposed are incompatible with the idea that an insurer is automatically discharged from liability from the date of the breach. Section 33(3) states that ...subject to any express provision in the policy, the insured is discharged from liability as from the date of the breach of warranty, but without prejudice to any liability incurred by him before that date. If an insurer is automatically discharged from liability from the date of the breach, it cannot logically be liable to pay a subsequent loss unconnected with the breach.

If one were to repeal section 33(3) it would be necessary to put something in its place. If not, the repeal would only lead to confusion about how far the provision merely reflected the pre-existing common law position, which continued unchanged. The question is how far any statutory restatement should go in altering the current law.

If warranties are not to be given any special or pre-eminent status, then it would be more in keeping with general contractual principles to provide that a breach by one party merely gave the other party the choice. When an injured party becomes aware of the breach, it may either decide to repudiate the contract or to affirm it and continue with the relationship.

Should the reforms provide that a breach of warranty gives the insurer the right to repudiate the contract, rather than automatically discharging it from liability?

In 1980 the Law Commission argued that the issue of past claims and future repudiation should be treated separately. An insurer should be able to pay past claims and repudiate the policy for the future; it should also be entitled to reject claims, without repudiating in the future.

Under the tentative proposals in this paper, a breach of warranty would mean that an insurer was not liable for a loss causally connected to the breach (though, as we discuss below, it would be possible for the insurer to waive this breach). The breach would not affect any past unconnected losses. However, the question is whether the breach should also entitle an insurer to choose to bring the policy to an end. This means that the insurer would no longer be liable to meet any claims (whether causally connected to the breach or not) from the time the decision was communicated to the insured,

Should the reforms provide an insurer with a choice between repudiating the claim only, or the policy for the future, or both? The implications of termination: liability for premiums, notice and waiver.

If the reforms were to provide that a breach of warranty gives an insurer the right to bring a contract to an end, this raises three further questions. First, should the insured continue to be liable to pay premiums after the contract is terminated? Secondly, should the insurer's right to repudiate for the future be subject to a requirement to give reasonable notice? Finally, what effect would this have on the law of waiver? We explore these issues below.

FUTURE PREMIUMS

Under general contract law, where one party accepts the other's wrongful repudiation, the effect is to bring to an end both parties' primary obligations under the contract. As Lord Diplock put it: (a) there is substituted by implication of law for the primary obligations of the party in default which remain unperformed a secondary obligation to pay money compensation to the other party for the loss sustained by him in consequence of their non-performance in the future and (b) the unperformed primary obligations of that other party are discharged.

This means that neither the innocent nor the guilty party are required to perform any further primary obligations under the contract (though ancillary clauses, dealing with matters such as arbitration, may survive). If the guilty party has been paying by instalments, the normal rule is that the insured remains liable for any payments that fall due before the repudiation is accepted, but not for payments due after that date. The primary obligation to pay the instalments is replaced with a secondary obligation to pay damages for loss of profits. This contrasts with the rule for breach of warranty under section 33(3), under which only the insurer is discharged from liability: the insured remains liable to pay future instalments of the premium. As we have seen, under the current law if the insured breaches a payment of premium warranty, the insurer is automatically discharged from further liability, but the insured must continue to make payments.

The question is what would happen if we were to repeal section 33(3) and replace it with an insurer's right to accept repudiation? It is unclear whether the normal rule would apply, so that the insured would cease to be liable for the premium). The insurer might be able to argue that the separate instalments did not constitute different payments for divisible periods of cover (with, for example, each monthly instalment paying for each month's cover). Instead, it could be said that the premium was one single indivisible payment for one single period of cover: it was just that the contract permitted the single premium to be paid over the course of time.

This latter argument was accepted in *Chapman v Kardirga*. Chadwick LJ commented: the Judge [at first instance] was wrong to hold that the effect of the payment of premium clause [which allowed payment by quarterly instalments]...was to apportion the premium payable under the policy to discreet periods of the term of the policy; that is to say, to convert what was (but for the payment of premiums clause) a premium payable in respect of the entire risk into a series of premiums payable in respect of risks during successive periods...The fact that the successive instalments are due and payable on dates which occur at three monthly intervals during the term of the policy does not, in my view, lead to the conclusion that the premium, which comprises the aggregate of those instalments, is itself divisible between successive three month intervals.

If it were accepted that the premium became due immediately (with payment postponed into instalments) then the insured would remain liable to pay the whole premium even after the repudiation was accepted. We do not think that this result would be fair. It would allow the insurer to make a windfall profit from the insured's breach of warranty, by keeping the premiums and not incurring any liability. In our view, the normal default rule should be that the insured would no longer be liable to pay premium instalments that fell due after the contract has been terminated.

Is it agreed that if the insurer accepts the insured's breach of warranty, so as to terminate future liability, the insured should cease to be liable for future premiums?

PREMIUMS PAID IN ADVANCE

A more difficult question is what should happen if the insured has paid the premium in advance. Under normal contract principles, the insured would only be entitled to the return of the premium if there had been a total failure of consideration.48 For this, the breach, and the acceptance of the breach, must have occurred before the cover started.

However, for many types of contract, the courts are prepared to divide the bargain into constituent parts. Where some of the advance payment can be attributed to a particular part of the contract, and the consideration for that part has wholly failed, the guilty party may recover that portion of money. This would apply in a yearly insurance contract where it was possible to divide the total cover into 12 separate monthly parts. It would mean that if a breach of warranty were accepted in Month 2, the insured would be entitled to be repaid 10/12ths of the advance premium, less any damages due to the insurer for administrative expenses and loss of profit.

The question is whether this is a desirable result. We are keen to improve communication and trust between insurers and insured, and we are concerned that allowing the insurer to retain the whole premium may operate to undermine such trust. Suppose, for example, a shop owner has warranted that the shop will be protected by a working burglar alarm at all times, and the burglar alarm breaks down. Ideally, the shop owner would contact the insurer to tell them about the problem as soon as possible. However, if this would permit the insurer to cancel the policy and retain ten months' premium, the owner would be better off keeping quiet. They might calculate that the alarm would be fixed soon, before any loss happens. Furthermore, under our reforms, the insurer would remain liable for losses unconnected with the problem, giving the insured a clear incentive not to alert the insurer.

We would be interested to hear views on whether an insurer who terminates a policy following the insured's breach of warranty should normally provide a pro-rata refund of the outstanding premium, less any damages or administrative costs.

Notice

Under our proposals, once an insurer had communicated its acceptance of the breach to the insured, it would no longer be liable for future claims. This would not make any difference to claims for losses connected to the breach (for which the insurer would not be liable in any event) but it would terminate all the insurer's other liability for claims arising after the effective date. This leads to the question whether the insurer should give reasonable notice of such a termination. Should the termination take place when it is received, or only after sufficient time for the insured to make other arrangements?

In Australia, the insurer cannot bring a contract to an end as a result of the breach, but it is entitled to terminate the contract using a cancellation clause. Under section 59 of the Insurance Contracts Act 1984, the insurer must give at least three days notice in writing. In Norway, circumstances covered by a warranty would normally be considered as an alteration in the risk. This would permit the insurer to terminate the contract, but only after 14 days notice.

We think that a requirement for a period of reasonable notice would encourage insureds to report breaches of warranty. If a notice period is to be specified, it should reflect a reasonable period for the insured to make other arrangements. We would welcome views about whether this is more likely to be a few days or a couple of weeks, or somewhere in between.

We welcome views as to whether the act should include any requirement for notice. If so, what would constitute a reasonable time for an insured to make other arrangements?

Waiver and Affirmation

The changes we have proposed to section 33 of the MIA 1906 would have consequences for the law on waiver. The 1906 Act specifically states that "a breach of warranty may be waived by the insurer". However, since the House of Lords decision in *The Good Luck*, there has been a considerable academic debate over how breaches of warranty may be waived.

In English contract law, there are two ways in which a party may be taken to have waived their rights when faced with the other party's repudiatory breach.54 The first way is by making a choice between two inconsistent courses of action. The wronged party has a choice: either to treat the breach as discharging the contract (ie to "repudiate" or "terminate" the contract), or to affirm the contract. If they affirm, it seems the right to repudiate will be lost provided that the wronged party knew of the facts giving rise to the right to repudiate and, it would appear, that they possessed the right in question. The wronged party must then evince a decision to relinquish that right by words or conduct. Once the party has made the choice to affirm the contract, it is bound by that decision. This type of waiver is sometimes called "waiver by election".

The second way is through "waiver by estoppel". This requires the wronged party to make an unequivocal representation by words or conduct that it will not rely on its legal rights. The other party must show that it relied on the representation by doing something or refraining from doing something, in circumstances where it would be inequitable for the wronged party to rely on its legal rights. Normally, the other party would have to show that it has altered its position to its own detriment.

Often both forms of waiver involve similar types of inconsistent acts. For example, after learning of a breach an insurer may accept premiums, or issue a policy document, or handle a claim. For affirmation, the issue would be whether the insurer had the requisite knowledge and whether the act shows that it intended to continue with the policy. For "waiver by estoppel" the focus shifts to the policyholder's perceptions and conduct. Did the act appear to show that the insurer did not intend to rely on its legal rights? If so, did the policyholder in fact rely on this representation by, for example, failing to take out another insurance policy? It is usually more difficult for the policyholder to show waiver by estoppel because it has to prove that it relied on the representation, usually to its detriment. The policyholder would not need to prove that the insurer knew that it had the right to deny liability, but the policyholder would need to show that a reasonable policyholder in their position would think that the insurer was aware of the right.

It is now thought, following *The Good Luck*, that affirmation, or waiver by election, is not applicable to a breach of an insurance warranty of assurance. In *HIH*

Casualty & General Insurance Ltd v AXA Corporate Solutions, Lord Justice Tuckey explained with apparent approval the reasoning of the trial judge:61 where there is a breach of warranty there is no scope for traditional waiver by election because the insurer is automatically discharged from liability upon breach and therefore has no choice to make. This is why only waiver by estoppel availed HIH, if it did...

This puts a heavier burden on the policyholder as they not only have to show that the insurer made an unequivocal representation, but also that they relied on it.

Scots law has not developed a classification equivalent to the English law distinction between waiver by election and waiver by estoppel. The decision of the House of Lords in *Armia Ltd v Daejan Developments Ltd*63 has generally been regarded as authority for the proposition that a party relying on the other party's abandonment of a right must demonstrate that he has conducted his affairs on the basis of the waiver, although he need not go so far as to show that he has suffered prejudice as a consequence of relying upon it. In reaching this decision, the House of Lords referred to certain English authorities while cautioning that the Scots law of personal bar should not be assumed to be the same as the English law of estoppel.

We think that if the change we have suggested to section 33 is put into effect, so that the contract is not discharged automatically by a breach of warranty but the insurer has the right to repudiate (or, as some prefer to say, terminate) for breach, whether the insurer is precluded by its subsequent conduct from exercising that right can be left to the general law of contract. Thus in English law, for example, the insurer might lose its right by either affirmation or estoppel. We think this is just. There is a case for allowing an insured to found upon a waiver by the insurer without having to show that they relied on the representation.

Particularly in the case of an express statement by the insurer who is aware of the breach that it does not insist upon its rights consequent upon the breach of warranty, it is difficult to see why an additional requirement of proving reliance should be imposed upon the insured. The same may be said where the waiver is clear from actions of the insurer.

We do not think it is necessary to include a specific provision on this point in any new legislation, but we would welcome views on the point.

We tentatively propose that Marine Insurance Act 1906, section 33(2) should be repealed. Loss by waiver of the insurer's right to repudiate the contract would in future be determined in accordance with the general rules of contract. We welcome views on whether it is necessary to include a specific provision on this point in any new legislation.

11

AN UNFAIR TERMS APPROACH TO COMMERCIAL INSURANCE

In this chapter we have discussed ways in which warranties and unexpected definitions of the risk hidden within contractual small print may be used to produce results that are unfair to policyholders. As we have seen, consumer insurance is subject to the Unfair Terms in Commercial Contracts Regulations 1999, which require terms that go beyond the main definition of the subject matter to be fair. We have suggested that unexpectedly narrow definitions of the risk and unexpectedly wide exclusions can be challenged under the Regulations. However, there is no similar protection for commercial insurance.

In other areas of commercial life, businesses are given protection against unfair terms by the Unfair Contract Terms Act 1977 (UCTA). When a business is dealing on its written standard terms of business, it cannot rely on a clause as entitling it to render a contractual performance substantially different from that which was reasonably expected, or to render no performance at all, unless the clause is fair and reasonable. However UCTA does not apply to insurance contracts.

For the purposes of this paper, we are primarily interested in whether an unfair terms approach could be substituted for the causal connection test outlined in Part 7, or added to it to deal with clauses that define the risk or provide exceptions to the cover.

As we have seen, we do not think that the causal connection test should apply only to warranties, but should extend to all clauses that define the risk. This, however, may be over-inclusive. We suggest that it should be subject to a proviso to allow the insurer to escape liability where the activity is so far outside the terms of the cover that a reasonable insured could not have expected the loss to be covered. A more direct approach may be to look at the fairness of the term. Thus the causal connection test might be confined to warranties, and other exclusions could be subject to a fairness test. Alternatively, the warranty itself might be subjected to the test of fairness if the insurer attempted to rely on it to render a performance that was substantially different from what the insured reasonably expected. The fairness test might apply to all standard term business insurance contracts, or might be confined to those entered into by small businesses.

It is possible that unfair terms protection could also be applied to other problematic terms in insurance contracts. In the first issues paper we raised the question of whether insurers should only be permitted to exclude our proposed reforms on misrepresentation and non-disclosure in small business contracts in so far as this was fair. In subsequent papers we intend to return to the question of notification clauses: one answer to the problems they cause might be to subject them to a test of fairness. In this paper, however, we raise general questions about an unfair terms approach only in relation to warranties, definitions of the risk and exclusions.

Here we begin by outlining the effect of sections 3 and 17 of UCTA on other types of commercial contract. We then consider the arguments for and against extending this protection to commercial insurance.

THE UNFAIR CONTRACT TERMS ACT 1977, SECTIONS 3 & 17

In England and Wales, section 3 subjects certain clauses to a requirement of reasonableness. It applies between contracting parties where one of them deals as a consumer or on the other's written standard terms of business. Section 3(2)(b) prevents the party who wrote the standard terms of business from claiming to be entitled

(i) to render a contractual performance substantially different from that which was reasonably expected of him, or

(ii) in respect of the whole or any part of his contractual obligation, to render no contractual performance at all, except in so far as... the contract term satisfies the requirement of reasonableness.

In Scotland, the issue is dealt with by section 17, which enacts the same substantive provision, using slightly different words. It provides that a term in a consumer contract or standard form contract "shall have no effect for the purpose of enabling a party to a contract...(b) in respect of a contractual obligation, to render no performance, or to render a performance which is substantially different from that which the consumer or customer reasonably expected from the contract if it was not fair and reasonable to incorporate the term in the contract.

In February 2005, the two Law Commissions produced a joint report and draft Bill to amend the law of unfair contract terms. As far as sections 3 and 17 are concerned, we did not intend to make any substantive changes in the law. However, we aimed to produce a single section to apply to the whole of Great Britain, written in clearer language.

Clause 9(3) of the draft Bill applies where one party to a business contract ("A") deals on the written standard terms of business of the other ("B"). It states that Unless the term is fair and reasonable, B cannot rely on any of those terms to claim it has the right – (a) to carry out its obligations under the contract in a way substantially different from the way in which A reasonably expected them to be carried out, or (b) not to carry out all or part of those obligations.

These provisions require the court to start with three questions:

(1) What contractual performance did A reasonably expect?

(2) What contractual performance does B claim to be entitled to render?

(3) Is there a substantial difference between the two?

Is so, the court must then ask whether the term satisfies the requirement of reasonableness, given the circumstances that were or ought to have been in the contemplation of the parties when the contract was made.

The first question must be approached broadly as a matter of fact. As Lord Bingham pointed out in *Zockoll Group Ltd v Mercury Communications Ltd,* the "answer cannot depend on the proper construction of the contract".3 If a party could only reasonably expect that which the contract actually provided there would never be any discrepancy between the two. Instead, in a case such as *Kler Knitwear* the court would need to start by asking whether the claimants reasonably expected that, if they were late in checking the sprinkler system, claims for storm damage would be paid. If so, the court would then ask whether this was what the contract in fact provided? If not, was the difference substantial? After this initial hurdle has been cleared, the court would then need to consider whether the clause introducing a warranty was fair at the time the contract was made.

Industry Standard Terms

A difficult question about UCTA is how it applies to industry standard wording. In our 2005 report we discussed the meaning of "written standard terms of business". If one party regularly uses industry standard terms, and puts them forward for the contract in question, then it is probable that they would be caught by sections 3 and 17. During consultation, several consultees suggested that there should be a special exemption for terms drafted by a trade association. However, we decided against such an exemption: The reason is that there can be no guarantee that terms will be fair simply because they were drawn up by a third party and are used widely in the relevant market. The terms might have been drawn up by a trade association that represents the interests of one party and not those of the other party; and yet may be used in the vast majority of contracts in the market because, for example, the other party usually lacks the sophistication or the bargaining power to demand terms more favourable to it.

Although there would not be a blanket exemption, however, the provenance of the terms and the degree to which they are excepted in the market would be highly relevant to any decision about whether they are reasonable. If terms are the result of genuine negotiation by both sides of the market acting on equal terms, it is very unlikely that a court will find them to be unfair.

THE ARGUMENTS FOR EXTENSION

We do not think that extending sections 3 and 17 and their replacement to insurance would make any difference to consumer contracts. As discussed earlier, the Unfair Terms in Consumer Contract Regulations already require that a term must be fair, if it enables the insurer to render a contractual performance substantially different from that which was reasonably expected. Furthermore, in 1990, the Insurance Ombudsman stated that he would apply the spirit of the Unfair Contract Terms Act 1977, and the Financial Ombudsman Service has continued this tradition. However, the section would give substantially improved rights to small and medium businesses that are forced to contract on the insurer's standard terms of business.

We see three main advantages in extending sections 3 and 17 of the Unfair Contract Terms Act 1977 to insurance contracts:

(1) The protection only applies to standard term contracts. It does not interfere with the freedom of large businesses to negotiate contracts on an individual basis. We would prefer to make a distinction on the basis of how the contract was negotiated rather than attempt to find some other proxy for those who need protection and those who do not, such as size or nature of the business.

(2) It applies to any term that defines cover in a way that policyholders would not reasonably expect, and to any term that allows the insurer not to pay a claim at all. Unlike section 54 of the Australian Insurance Contracts Act 1984, it looks at the substance of the term rather than its form. It therefore avoids the sort of semantic distinctions between, for example, "omissions" and "inactions" that have bedevilled section 54. In the case of claims made and notified policies, for example, the court would start with looking at what policyholders would reasonably expect. If the insurance had been sold in such a way that the policyholder should have realised that it was limited to claims made and notified during the

contractual period, that would be the end of the matter. But if a "condition precedent" were written in such a way that an insurer could avoid paying a claim for which they were otherwise liable for a trivial delay, the court would need to examine how far the clause was fair and reasonable.

(3) In examining whether a term was fair and reasonable, the court would need to take into account both the extent to which the term was transparent and its substance and effect. This means that a term written in plain language and brought to the policyholder's attention would be much less likely to be found to be unfair than one lost in obscure small print. The reform would provide a strong incentive to insurers to re-write their contractual documents in a way that policyholders understand.

THE ARGUMENTS AGAINST EXTENSION

Freedom of Contract

The first argument is that controls on unfair contract terms interfere with freedom of contract. A dynamic and innovative market is best served if the parties are allowed to agree what they want.

This argument was put to the joint Law Commissions when we recommended the controls in 1975.6 In 1975 we replied that: It is valid only to the extent that there is true freedom of contract to interfere with, and the objection has no validity where there is no real possibility of negotiating contract terms, or where a party is not expected to read a contract carefully or to understand its implications without legal advice.

It is of course difficult to distinguish between situations where there is genuine freedom of contract and those where there is not. The fact that the contract is on standard terms suggests that freedom is limited. We also thought that the strength of the bargaining positions of the parties and their understanding of the term in question should be taken into account in a test of reasonableness.

Uncertainty

The second argument is that it introduces unacceptable uncertainty into the law. The insurance industry also put them with great force when it secured an exception from the Unfair Contract Terms Act in 1977.

Before the 1977 Act was passed, fears were expressed that it would lead to great uncertainty and an unacceptable level of litigation. A problem with UCTA is that it can be used for its "nuisance potential".

In other words, debtors can buy more time in which to pay debts by putting in weak defences, claiming that terms are unfair even if they were readily agreed to at the time. However, this is less likely to be a problem with insurance, where the onus will be on the policyholder to bring the claim. There are already many deterrents to stop small and medium businesses from bringing weak claims against insurers.

In practice, UCTA has generated only moderate amounts of litigation. Sections 3 and 17 have become generally accepted, and in our recent review of the legislation we received no demands for their repeal. It must be remembered that the existing law is extremely uncertain: there is a danger that cases raising the same issues as *Kler Knitwear* will be litigated repeatedly, as insurers test out new and better wording to remove any possibility of ambiguity.

We would consider this option only if it were really needed. There would need to be evidence that businesses require better protection not only against warranties but also against unexpectedly narrow definitions of the risk or unexpectedly wide exceptions, and that the approach which we advocate in Part 7 is unacceptable. If the only real problems are encountered by small businesses, the protection could be confined to small businesses (though this raises questions of definition discussed in the first Issues Paper). We would welcome further advice on whether such protection is needed, and what the consequences might be.

We invite views on whether clauses that define the risk and exclusions in business insurance contracts written on the insurers' standard terms should be subject to a test of fairness and, if so, whether the protection should apply to all businesses or only those defined as small.

BIBLIOGRAPHY

Arrow, Kenneth J.: *Social Choice and Individual Values,* New York, Wiley, 1951.

Campbell, J.Y., Lo, A.W.: *The Econometrics of Financial Markets,* Princeton University Press, 1996.

Chaudhuri, Pramit: *The Indian Economy: Poverty and Development,* New York, St. Martin's Press, 1979.

Dhingra, C.: *The Indian Economy: Resources, Planning, Development, and Problems,* Delhi, Sultan Chand, 1983.

Greer, Douglas F.: *Industrial Organization and Public Policy,* MacMillan Publishing Company, 1992.

Ishwar, C.: *The Indian Economy: Resources, Planning, Development, and Problems,* Delhi, Sultan Chand, 1983.

Little, I.M.D.: *India: Macroeconomics and Political Economy, 1964-1991,* Washington, World Bank, 1994.

Mongia, J.N.: *India's Economic Development Strategies, 1951-2000 A.D..* New Delhi, Allied, 1986.

Pranab, K.: *The Political Economy of Development in India,* Delhi, Oxford University Press, 1984.

Sargent, Thomas J.: *Dynamic Macroeconomic Theory.* Harvard University Press, 1987.

Tirole, Jean: *The Theory of Industrial Organization,* MIT Press, 1988.

Williamson, Jeffrey G.: *American Inequality: A Macroeconomic History,* New York, Academic Press, 1980.

Xavier Sala-i-Martin: *Economic Growth.* McGraw-Hill, 1995.

INDEX

classic

1998
16